THE CASE FOR CAPITAL PUNISHMENT

Alfred B. Heilbrun Jr.

Hamilton Books
A member of
The Rowman & Littlefield Publishing Group
Lanham · Boulder · New York · Toronto · Plymouth, UK

Copyright © 2013 by
Hamilton Books
4501 Forbes Boulevard
Suite 200
Lanham, Maryland 20706
Hamilton Books Acquisitions Department (301) 459-3366

10 Thornbury Road
Plymouth PL6 7PP
United Kingdom

Library of Congress Control Number: 2012950207
ISBN: 978-0-7618-6035-8
eISBN: 978-0-7618-6036-5

To my wife, Marian,
and our adult children
Kirk, Lynn, Kim, Leigh and Mark

Contents

Contents

Preface

There is a serious need for an informed controversy in this country regarding the death penalty as a mechanism of criminal justice. Instead, it strikes me that the wide differences of opinions take on stealth qualities, and the general public remains uninformed when it comes to the real issues surrounding capital punishment.

At one divergent extreme we find those who oppose the death penalty on moral grounds. They reason that executing a criminal for a serious crime represents intentional killing by the state. This is viewed as violating a cardinal moral principle—in biblical terms, "thou shalt not kill." Support for this view is most likely to reach the public in the guise of cryptic news items that offer little perspective on the issue of capital punishment. Within recent memory I have encountered a news brief regarding a governor who placed a moratorium on executions in his state as a matter of conscience. A legislative body in another state chose to drop the death penalty altogether. A judge elsewhere ruled that a capital punishment sentence imposed 18 years earlier was too harsh; the prisoner was resentenced to life without parole. Such actions as these erode the justification for capital punishment in American jurisprudence without weighing the pros and cons of the issue.

Facing off against those who oppose the death penalty on moral grounds is another faction that favors this extreme punishment with equal fervor. Justice for them requires that a criminal who has intentionally taken a life and has done so in an especially deplorable way should be punished by execution—in biblical terms, "an eye for an eye". Those who are committed to seeking justice for the victim of an intentional killing are no more likely to be invested in weighing the pros and cons of their view than those who are opposed to this sentence. Execution is either unacceptable, on the one hand, or mandatory on the other.

Somewhere between the extremes of those who oppose the death penalty for moral reasons and others who support its use as a way of seeking justice for the victim is the social pragmatist. The pragmatic approach would be to determine whether capital punishment provides an undeniable social benefit to the society at large that goes beyond the satisfaction of those at the extremes of preference. That is what this book is all about—trying to establish whether a society gains some clear-cut advantage by exacting the most severe punishment for the most serious crime?

It also was important that the decision regarding pragmatic value should depend upon scientific research. The methods of social science can be woefully out of place in examining emotionally-tinged responses to the death penalty whether they are associated with rejection on moral grounds or approval based on justice for the victim. However, answering a question on pragmatic value is another matter. This book describes a study that focuses upon what is certainly among the most useful social benefits that could be delivered by a criminal justice mechanism, the deterrence of future intentional killing. The pragmatic value of capital punishment will be weighed by the evidence found in pursuing two questions. Would a state experience less future willful killing after adopting the death penalty? Conversely, would that state see an increase in willful killing in its future if the death penalty were legally compromised or abolished?

Chapter 1

The Background for Considering the Death Penalty Controversy

The moral codes and subsequent formal legal statutes governing punishment for misbehaviors since the arrival of the earliest settlers in North America have always included the death penalty for the most serious violations. The one brief exception to this tradition, between 1968 and 1976, will play a critical role in the study of capital punishment to be described in the next chapter. The manner in which lethal punishment is inflicted has evolved from stoning or burning at the stake for moral transgressions. More recent forms of execution have involved hanging, electrocution, and various forms of lethal injections for the most serious forms of violence. Efforts to turn an inherently cruel act, taking the life of an unwilling prisoner, into a more humane procedure has not been particularly successful judging by those who oppose the death penalty. The right of the state to take the life of a criminal continues to be challenged no matter how egregious the crime or how execution is effected.

A variety of law-related reasons are cited for opposing the execution of prisoners that range from trivial (the state serving as a violent model for its residents) to important (irreversible error when the executed person is later found to be innocent of a capital offense). Perhaps the most commonplace reason for rejecting the death penalty is a moral repugnance toward intentional killing in one or more of its common guises—state-sanctioned execution, national military action, abortion. In opposition to intentional killing resides the basic irony of the debate between those who oppose capital punishment and those who favor it. Oppositionists strongly reject the taking of a human life but so do those who favor the death penalty. In the opposition case the concern is over executing the person who almost inevitably has been convicted of murder under egregious circumstances. For those favoring capital punishment the object of concern is the victim of the crime who presumably has not provoked lethal violence.

Rather than trying to resolve this moral issue as it stands, this book and the study it describes took a different tack. The question became whether the death penalty can make a positive social contribution that outweighs the values implicit in either of the contrasting moral positions on execution? The evidence will take us beyond whether it is right or wrong to execute the individual convicted of a capital crime or if it is right or wrong to seek justice by avenging the death of the individual victim? Rather, the emphasis will be on whether the threat of execution for taking a life reduces the risk of becoming a murder victim within the broader society. The emphasis, then, will be on the protection of future victims rather than the punishment of the individual criminal.

Conclusions regarding the pragmatic value of capital punishment will be based upon a study published six years ago (Heilbrun, 2006) in which I traced the murder rate across the United States from 1958 to 2003. The purpose of this survey was to determine whether the existence of a law allowing the death penalty had either or both of two effects. One effect was the rate of killing. The other was the number of victims in a given state. The procedure followed in the study and the results of the investigation will be described in forthcoming chapters.

I realize that the average reader is not accustomed to having conclusions about capital punishment presented in the context of social science methodology nor is the reader likely to have quantitative data made available that can be used to support these conclusions. More than likely, current judgments of the readers about the death penalty will be based upon media reports. From my experience such information seems to emphasize biographical background of the criminal, description of the crime, and the quality of the evidence in the case. What often comes through in these selective accounts of capital punishment is concern over a particular execution and over this form of punishment in general.

This book will give the reader a chance to take a more informed look at the death penalty, present or absent, over the entire nation and over an extended period of time. I will present the method and results of the study in as understandable way as I can and will include the "warts and blemishes" that social science inevitably demonstrates. Imperfections are especially prevalent when the topic is complicated and the method of investigation required goes beyond simple correlation (when A goes up, B goes up or down). Please believe me when I say that the topic under consideration is a lot more complex than you would expect if you have been exposed to moral precepts in settling the issue. I will try to do my part by making the procedures of the study intelligible and my conclusions a reasonable fit to the data. Readers can do their part by accepting the possibility of complication for the moment. Keep in mind that the best understanding generated by social science research requires that you allow for exceptions and grant conditional relationships.

Crime and Punishment

The criminal justice system in this country is predicated upon a philosophy of graduated increments of punishment as the severity of the individual's unlawful behaviors increases. Severity is judged principally by amount of harm to a victim, although other factors may enter into the punishment. This appears to be about the only just way to maintain a system of punishment, and most would probably agree with that conclusion. Where you would begin to find some disagreement is in what form the punishment should take, although imprisonment is the prevalent form with length of incarceration used for differentiating severity of offense.

There is also disagreement regarding what is to be accomplished by keeping an offender in prison. Is it to be regarded as *punishment*, pure and simple, with the criminal suffering the deprivation of ordinary rights and exposure to the humiliation of being labeled a convict? Others might regard time in prison as a form of *isolation* in which people are protected from an individual who has proven to be a danger to society. A third more benevolent view is that placing someone in the controlled environment of a prison offers the opportunity for *rehabilitation* that will allow the prisoner to live constructively back in society.

These philosophies of imprisonment are not mutually exclusive, of course, and all are predicated upon the importance of concentrating upon the individual criminal in the effort to control unlawful behavior in society. The individual commits the crime, is tried and convicted, and then goes to prison with an eye to reducing the risk of further offenses.

Consideration of these philosophies of punishment have been included simply to help explain why crime and punishment are commonly understood in terms of a known individual associated with a particular crime. As long as guilt is established, that individual receives whatever punishment is justified by the crime less concessions made in reaching that outcome. The point here is that the "known individual" has a face, a name, and a social history that can elicit either positive or negative feelings. Knowing that an actual person is being considered makes punishment, isolation, or rehabilitation more tangible outcomes of criminal transgression.

A fourth possible way to avert crime by way of punishment is quite distinct from those who attempt to modify the known criminal so that he or she is less likely to prove a risk to society after leaving prison. This approach requires that we depend upon some type of punishment as a *deterrent* to some future crime by a potential criminal. That is not to say that incarceration or even monetary penalties do not reduce the risk of intentionally breaking the law. The crime rates in this country suggest that they leave something to be desired as deterrents, however. Furthermore, the crimes that will concern us in this book represent what most would agree are among the most horrendous violations of civilized conduct possible. Intentionally killing another person without provocation and doing so in a cruel and inhumane way is one example. Other egregious circumstances involving murder will be found in state statutes. The death penalty exists in 38 states and stands as the most formidable deterrent possible given that a person requires external threat to deter an antisocial act.

The question before us boils down to this. Does the possibility of receiving the death penalty for intentionally killing a victim in our society serve to reduce the risk that this type of crime will be less likely to occur in the future? Actually, a second question accompanies the first. Is the reduction in risk sufficient in lives saved to outweigh the cost in lives claimed by the death penalty?

Perhaps now I can contrast the essential differences between legal penalties imposed upon the known individual criminal and the death penalty as it will be considered as a deterrent to future crime. In focusing upon the individual criminal the crime is past, the criminal is known, and the long-term impact of prison is probably unknown. In examining the effect of the death penalty upon intentional killing, deterrence must precede the crime, the future criminals and victims are unknown, and the emphasis is upon the number of people who are spared becoming the murder victims. It may be in the reference to future unknown victims and in the use of quantitative terms that deterrence research may pale emotionally next to the accounts of executions and details of erroneous sentencing of known individuals. The prisoner depicted as a victim may be more compelling than statements such as ". . . 100 lives will be spared each year." Keep in mind that the number of people projected to be spared as victims over time when the murder rate drops or added as victims should the rate increase will be real enough even though their identity is unknown.

What is the Psychological Basis for Deterrence?

The dictionary tells us that to deter is "to prevent from action by fear of consequences." The deterrent in our present discussion of capital punishment is the fear that taking the life of another human (action) will result in execution by the state (consequence). This assumes that death-penalty statutes exist or at least the potential murderer thinks they do. After all, the fear is generated by the thought of impending consequences of an action and not by objective reality. This point becomes important as we consider what happens when death penalty states limit the information available to their residents about their capital punishment systems. Without awareness the fear of execution is not generated.

Another point to be made regarding the dictionary meaning of deterrence is that when an emotion such as fear serves as the motivational basis for human behavior, some variation of effect must be expected. People generally tend to dislike the experience of fear and will try to do whatever they can to eliminate that emotion. However, we can expect differing levels of this affect and some differences in the way that people will respond to the emotion. There are risk-takers among us as well as those who cannot get enough of roller-coaster rides or horror movies. The point here is that the fear generated by a deterrent would only be expected to prevent lethal action in some cases; others would not be deterred from acting by fear. The promising thing is that almost any improvement in our ability to deter intentional killing is magnified by the burgeoning population of the United States. Even a small decrease in murder rate in our country adds up to sparing thousands of lives. I have done the arithmetic.

Yet another point has considerable significance for psychological research. It bears upon the question of how you establish whether something like the death penalty has deterrence value? Early researchers, such as Sellin (1959), stipulated that two effects had to be observed in order to demonstrate deterrence by the death penalty: murder rate must *increase* when the death penalty is abolished and must *decrease* when the death penalty is restored. My sense of the research literature tells me that few researchers pay attention to demonstrating both required effects. They concentrate instead upon the dictionary sense of a deterrent as something that prevents action. However, the psychological principles governing abolishment and those governing restoration of capital punishment may not be the same, so it is safer to examine both conditions for their effect upon murder rate. The study you will be asked to consider offers an analysis of both abolishment and restoration of capital punishment as a more reliable procedure. As you will see, the psychological principles did turn out to be discrepant.

The study to be described ahead took advantage of a hiatus in executions and eventually even in the disappearance of the death penalty through the entire United States. The stoppages were long enough (1968–1976) and broad enough (all 50 states and the District of Columbia) to provide very reliable results when I looked at what happened to the rate of intentional killing after execution was halted. It was surprising to me that in the quarter century after the abolishment period ended in 1976, no one else had incorporated this gap as a way of more thoroughly examining deterrence effects in their research. At least I did not come across such a study. The rate of intentional killing was examined after the death penalty was restored in order to satisfy the second requirement of a deterrent.

What Type of Deterred Crime is Being Subjected to Investigation?

The ultimate relevance of the study to be described is whether capital punishment statutes in a state serve to deter the act of murder. That was not exactly what was investigated in the study and for good reason. The way that deterrence is typically studied by researchers, including me, does not really represent deterrence at all. We do not look directly at whether the anticipation of possible execution and the fear it engenders deters an intention to kill. This is very likely to be a private mental event that is not apparent to others and, if the person has any sense, will not be made known to others. True deterrence, then, is private and inaccessible to researchers.

What I have done to get around this impasse of inaccessibility is to use nondeterrence as an indicator of the importance of capital punishment in curbing intentional killing. The only assumptions required are logical. If there is a drop in murder rate, for example, when capital punishment is initiated, then it can be assigned value as a deterrent. By the same token, an increase in murder rate when the death penalty is abolished also is assumed to demonstrate its value as a deterrent. In other words, the failure to deter is studied. The only problem I see with this use of a correlate as a gauge of deterrent value is that it undoubtedly underestimates that value. I believe there are many more occasions when the fear of the death penalty *succeeds* and the person does not act on impulse (true deterrence) than when it *fails* and the person carries through with an intent to kill (nondeterrence) Actually, if one were dealing with the number of occasions when deterrence is successful, it should include the total number of occasions when the same individual blocks the impulse to kill for fear of execution. This means that if the evidence reported in the forthcoming study offers support to capital punishment as a deterrent to murder, the reader should feel free to consider that outcome as a conservative judgment.

The counts used in the deterrent study, then, depended upon the negative case. It would be the decrease in reported murders that would point to effectiveness of the death penalty as an inhibitor. It would be an increase in murders when there was no death penalty that would signal its importance as a disinhibitor. Both are important to defining deterrence. The number of murder or non-negligent manslaughter cases (both involving intentional killing and henceforth combined into "murder") reported by the police for each 100,000 people in a state's population, considered for each calendar year, provided a murder rate for the study. This murder rate is published annually by the Department of Justice. *Crime in the United States* includes this statistic for each state in the country along with the District of Columbia as well as many other pieces of vital information about criminal activity.

In summary, murder rate is based upon the number of intentional killings per 100,000 people in a state for a given year. The lower the number, the stronger the deterrence effect in that state assuming capital punishment statutes were in place. What I found when murder rate data were examined was that radical variation across states was the rule. Some states were found that had murder rates under 1 in 100,000 in a given year, whereas a murder rate as high as 20 in 100,000 was in evidence.

As the information from the Department of Justice accumulated, it became apparent that a second type of murder count would be informative. The absolute number of intentional slayings, also reported by the Department of Justice, is sensitive to the number of people in the state; the larger the population of the state, the more murders that will probably be reported. This is not automatically true for murder rate which is figured per 100,000 residents and is not arithmetically sensitive to total population differences The absolute number of intentional killings per state per year offers a better picture of how much each state contributes to the national murder problem. The murder rate is a better way to directly compare the murder problem in one state with that found in another.

States without capital punishment will serve as controls. Comparison with them will tell us whether the death penalty can be credited with deterrence value as the murder counts are considered. These methodological points in this section will be considered at greater length within the chapter that follows. I am trying to keep in mind that I should not overdo the discussion of scientific procedures and issues. It may seem to unduly delay getting to whatever answers the study is going to provide. My view, however, is that there are some controversies that require you to consider the quality of the research evidence in reaching a conclusion. Whether capital punishment should be a matter of law or not is certainly one of them.

One's position on the issue of capital punishment is frequently based on moral values that are more a matter of faith than evidence. Then too, these values are themselves in conflict on the matter. Should society seek "an eye for an eye" or heed the admonition "thou shalt not kill?" Attempts to influence others often assume an editorialized tone that fails to consider facts that either confirm or deny the message. Even the presumably objective view offered by social science requires caution, since it is difficult to escape the conclusion in examining some deterrence studies that the negative results were inevitable because of the simplistic and awkward method of investigation. With the present study I would like the reader to view the results as credible whatever they turn out to be, and awareness of procedures is the place to start.

Is Deterrence of an Impulse to Kill for Fear of Being Executed for the Crime the Same as an Act of Conscience?

How is this for an answer to the riddle above? To some extent they are the same. However, it depends upon how one defines deterrence and conscience, especially upon the psychological explanation one accepts with regard to how each works in preventing an act from occurring. That should not satisfy anyone as an answer; accordingly I will expand upon it to consider how fear as a deterrent and conscience overlap in meaning and how they differ as ways of governing antisocial behavior such as murder.

Deterrence already has received our attention as a way of governing homicidal behavior. Anticipation of harm to oneself, in this case execution by the state, arouses fear; the emotion of fear (and its unpleasant mental accompaniment) are aversive to the individual; the individual curbs the impulse to kill thereby reducing the aversive state—the fear and the mental accompaniment. Conscience has not been considered yet. The term generally describes the array of rights and wrongs assigned to overt behaviors by an individual and sometimes even the thought of these behaviors. Positive emotion results from behaving in the "right" way or not behaving in the "wrong" way. Negative emotion (guilt) results when the individual acts "wrong" or does not act "right." Right and wrong require quotation marks because they vary to some extent in substance and strength of conviction from person to person. The one commonly misunderstood quality of conscience is that the feelings of right and wrong must occur before the act in question to facilitate or deter the act to speak of conscience. A sense of right or wrong that are openly expressed after the act are most likely attempts to assuage guilt or manipulate others.

Does fear as a deterrent to willful killing and conscience ever overlap in function? My answer is in the affirmative but only to a very limited extent. If a conscientious person were to entertain the thought of killing someone, it is very likely that massive guilt would be generated before the act occurred. This would result in the suppression of the impulse as a way of relieving anticipatory guilt. In that case conscience would serve the same deterrent function as fear of consequences, but that is where the similarity ends. For one thing, guilt before a wrongful act goes well beyond simple fear of consequences to one self. It has much to do with issues of self-respect and the desire to please important others.

Going beyond the differences in psychological meaning for deterrence from fear and restraint by conscience is the fact that we are considering two very different types of people here. Those who refrain from willful killing because they fear the consequences to themselves and those who restrain themselves as a matter of conscience are almost mutually exclusive types of people. I have no evidence at hand, but I am convinced that when the deterrent effect of capital punishment is studied we are homing in on those with limited conscience. At least they are limited in the extent to which they experience anticipatory guilt before a very unacceptable act and depend upon fear of consequences to contain their actions.

Although the intentional killing count is far too high in our country, the truth of the matter is that most people do not need to depend upon the dire threat of the death penalty in order to avoid killing. They would experience this fear if it ever got that far, but the impulse to murder never gets beyond the shield of conscience. Accordingly, any deterrence effect promoted by capital punishment laws, as gauged by reduced murder rate and absolute murder count, will be provided by the people who are least responsive to self-governance as I see it. They are lacking in responsiveness to the dictates of conscience and must depend more upon external rewards and punishments to guide their behavior. Oh, yes! We can add to their midst the psychopaths who are not only lacking in an internalized conscience but are not particularly responsive to rights and wrongs dictated by society's laws. They *really* need the threat of execution to suppress an impulse to kill.

What is the Goal of this Book?

What I am trying to do in publishing this second look at my death-penalty study is to get information before the public that would be to their advantage and to that of the society at large. As far as I know, I missed the mark in my fist effort at accomplishing this. Too much was included in the book (Heilbrun 2006) beyond the essential features of background and research. I still want to examine the deterrence value of capital punishment with you in a research context, but I have cut back considerably on extraneous issues and added a new emphasis on collaborating variables. The first effort, by the way, is still worth a look when it comes to broader empirical coverage of lethal violence.

The conclusions in this book about the deterrence value of the death penalty may be enough to influence the opinion of the reader, and the fact that they have been presented in a research context, not in a popularized editorial, may contribute to this. A little activism never hurt anybody, and the public, after all, is the final arbiter of the laws that protect them.

Chapter 2

The Method of Study

In this chapter some of you are going to be introduced to the requirements of social science. The advantages of its findings over personal opinion or moral verdict, as long as these requirements are reasonably met, will hopefully be clear. Others who read this book are themselves social scientists and can understand the problems facing the researcher who attempts to tackle a problem that is both complex and subject to bias at every stage of investigation. Yes, social scientists do have personal biases that can influence not only how they interpret their results but why they select their problem and how they devise their methodology in the first place. I shall not refrain from pointing out examples of dubious methodology, although this is not going to turn into a hunting party in search of limitations in the way that others have examined deterrence.

Research Method

We are going to concentrate on four critical elements of a study in social science. Wait! Do not put this book back on the shelf quite yet. You need to understand these basics in order to judge the merit of my study or any study of deterrence by capital punishment. Not that many of you are then going to rush out to acquire the latest issue of *Law and Criminal Behavior*. At least though you may be in a better position to recognize that there is evidence on the subject and no need to depend upon someone's unsupported opinion. I shall use the methodology of my own study to explicate the four elements of social-science research; order is unimportant here.

Validity of Results Gained by Selecting Relevant Criteria

Validity has to do with whether the object of investigation is considered in a satisfactory way. As has been discussed, investigation of deterrence was conducted by examining murder rate and individual count of murders. Examination was limited by scientific necessity to the negative case—the failure to deter murder in a death-penalty state. The positive case, when deterrence is successful in a state with capital punishment, remains, by and large, an elusive private event inaccessible to the scientist. In the negative case a lower murder count suggests deterrence; a higher count in a state with the death penalty points to a weaker deterrent effect. Note the "weasel words" here. "Suggests" and "points to" are commonplace terms in social science, taking their place alongside "tends" and "indicates." Natural science has the luxury of laboratory procedures where greater precision is possible, but there are exceptions even there; think global warming as a natural-science phenomenon to be explained.

The criterion in a death-penalty deterrence study is the variable used to test for validity of a hypothesized relationship. In the deterrence study we are interested in the hypothesized relationship between capital punishment in a state and suppression of willful killing. The statistics on intentional killing (murder plus non-negligent manslaughter) are published yearly for each state and for Washington, D.C. by the U.S. Department of Justice based upon police input. These statistics provided the murder rate per 100,000 population in each state as well as the number of intentional-killing cases statewide. By using murder rate and taking total state population out of the picture, three things became possible: (1) deterrence in a large state could be compared to that in a small state; (2) deterrence in the same state could be compared over time as population changed; (3) states with differing populations could be combined to obtain an overall deterrence effect.

The absolute number of intentional killings offered a different way of examining deterrence effects. By bringing a state's total population back into the picture it was possible to gauge the contribution of that state's count of willful killings to the national problem with lethal violence.

It is difficult to see how murder rate or individual murder count can be criticized as criteria for deterrence on a state or national level. They conform closely to the meaning of deterrence that was under investigation. Both rate and count are provided by the agency best suited to gather crime statistics, the Department of Justice. This department uses the information generated by police forces who, in my opinion, are in the best position to analyze homicide cases without being required to make the legal compromises called for subsequently within our legal systems. Intentional killing remains a static judgment based upon available evidence.

The main way in which murder rate and individual count fall short in a validity sense is that they do not allow you access to deterrence in any direct way. The number of times that an individual has experienced an impulse to kill that is inhibited because the death penalty is feared cannot be measured scientifically. Yet each occasion would qualify as deterrence if such a count could be directly measured. In short, the murder counts I used provide a very conservative estimate of deterrence by capital punishment in my opinion.

Validity of Results Gained by Using a Control Condition

If a research condition is proposed to have a particular effect, as when the presence of state death-penalty statutes are thought to have a deterrent effect upon willful killing, the control condition would allow a parallel examination of willful killing in states that do not have capital punishment. The usual requirement of social science would be that the predicted deterrent effect would show up in the death-penalty states but would be less in the control states without capital punishment. This would lend confidence to the conclusion that deterrence had been revealed by the study. If the control condition showed the same effect over time as the death-penalty states, the same drop in intentional killing let us say, it would not be justified to claim a deterrence effect for capital punishment. A nationwide influence other than the death penalty would be suggested such as a general effort to suppress violence in some other way. The use of acceptable validity criteria or control conditions are not common in deterrence research. I can recall one research effort in which police chiefs were asked to give their judgments regarding whether capital punishment had an inhibiting effect upon intentional killing. The verdict was that it did not; chalk one up for those who are critical of the death penalty. Yet if you examine the method of study here, two things seem obvious to me. For one, no matter how experienced the police may be in the intricacies of criminal behavior, the many complexities of deterrence (more are yet to come in this book) are unlikely to be unraveled, even by chiefs of police. For another, where is the control condition for this kind of study?

Validity of Results Gained by Considering Confounded Variables

It may not be necessary to point out that several things can influence a proposed relationship in a social-science study between a predictor of interest and a criterion being predicted. In a deterrence study involving capital punishment, this would mean that there are several things that may influence the relationships between the fear generated by the death penalty and murder rate/individual murder count. These factors can be sources of error if they are overlooked, since they diminish the understanding of results. They may even mask the results to the point that a true relationship cannot be identified. I have designated these as "confounded variables" because their effects are intermixed with those of the variables being studied. They simply become part of the overall mass of the data. There is no way known to me beyond theoretical or common-sense speculation to be sure that all of the important confounded variables have been identified in a study bearing upon the social behavior of humans. Perhaps that is why rats were so popular as research subjects years ago.

If there is still some mystery about what I am talking about here, let me offer some specifics about the confounded variables that were fortunately isolated in the deterrence study. I will assure you ahead of time that it was *very* fortunate that they were identified and amenable to measurement. This made the conclusions easier to reach and seemingly more valid. Here are three.

The first confounded variable that proved valuable in clarifying the results was buried within the history of execution for the 38 states that were considered death-penalty states in the deterrence study. In a survey released by the Death Penalty Information Center of Southern Methodist University it was evident that over the 27 years that inhibition was studied (1977–2003) these states varied widely in their commitment to their own capital punishment systems. The states were broken down into high and low groups by number of executions to determine whether the effectiveness of the death penalty as a deterrent depended upon how seriously it was pursued. A good deal more about this confounded variable (as well as the next two to be described in brief) will be found on later pages.

A second confounded variable was suggested when state population numbers taken from census reports were considered. Interest was directed to whether intentional killing was not only more prevalent in count within larger states (which would not be a big surprise) but also in rate per 100,000. The question here was in whether the more congested environs of a high population state lends itself to more interpersonal strife and subsequent intentional killing. The answer to this question bears upon a very important issue in considering deterrence value. Do some states, those that are more highly populated, face an especially arduous task when they attempt to curb willful killing? If so, deterrence would be an uphill struggle for them.

The third confounded variable was evident within the state population counts. What percentage of the total population was made up of minorities? The census data were consulted to determine whether the percentage of minorities in a white-majority state was associated with a greater incidence of willful killing. Since large-population states tend to have higher percentages of minority residents, the question became whether there was a convergent importance of the two confounded population variables as far as the frequency of intentional killing was concerned. The size of the state population and the magnitude of the minority percentage were considered together as indicators of how difficult the goal of deterrence would prove to be.

That I would even check the possible role of minority presence in a state as a possible determinant of intentional killing might offend some. It is not necessary to assume that the danger resides in either the white majority or in the minorities. Prejudice can cut either way as can criminal misbehavior.

However, concern about blame should not prevent a more general inquiry into whether the presence of a higher minority representation is associated with an increase in intentional killing and a special deterrence problem.

Reliability—the Stability of Results

No matter what results are achieved in a scientific study, it is still important to assume that at least similar results can be obtained if the same research conditions and procedures are replicated. Without stable findings an investigation has no value. This is more a problem for social science than some other sciences, since it primarily concerns itself with human social behavior. Social behavior, which is often interpersonal in nature, shows considerable variability compared to other aspects of our environment. This can be explained by the fact that there are so many determinants of a social act that are unknown (or that may go unmeasured even if known) that the way is open to limited reliability. If the unknown or unmeasured determinants of a social act vary from one time to the next, variation in findings would be expected—unreliability.

Since the problem of unreliability is a commonplace concern in psychological research, it is fair to ask what psychologists do to maintain confidence in our findings? Just a few alternatives may suffice. In small-sample research where subjects are limited in number, we take our findings and by prescribed statistical tests and probability tables determine whether the odds of finding them by chance are less than 5 in 100 say. Life does not offer much better odds than that so you accept the results as reliable. Another approach is to repeat your study to see if you get the same results. Not many do that. Finally, use extremely large samples of subjects—so large in fact that it is hard to imagine that the results of a study are not stable. This is the approach to reliable results in the deterrence study with subject numbers in the millions, all states (plus the District of Columbia) included, and a time frame for studying deterrence extended to 46 years.

The Deterrence Study

Now that the reader has been exposed to some of the primary requisites of research in social science (and some of its limitations) we can move on to why this is important to the topic at hand. I intend to present a study of capital punishment as a deterrent to intentional killing in the United States that provides a conclusion based upon worthwhile evidence. In addition, the study will include some considerations that are rarely encountered in death-penalty deterrence studies.

The deterrence study ahead hinged upon what could be considered glitches in our judicial system at the highest level. Between 1968 and 1971 a number of Supreme Court cases regarding juries in death-penalty trials were heard; the decisions led to a halt in executions throughout the country. States with capital punishment awaited a clearer perspective on the constitutionality of sentencing in capital cases for fear of reversal of the sentence. Issues before the court included: whether prospective jurors could be excluded from capital cases if they held reservations about the death penalty; whether the death penalty could be reached only by a jury (and not by a judge); whether there were uniform standards for assigning the death penalty; and whether separate guilt and penalty phases were needed in a capital case. The nationwide hold on executions in death-penalty states and the increased concern among prosecutors over seeking the death penalty contributed to a weakening of capital punishment over this four-year *moratorium* period.

In 1972 the walls came down on the death penalty in the United States as the Supreme Court found this form of punishment unconstitutional, in violation of the Eighth ("cruel and unusual punishment") and Fourteenth ("due process") Amendment rights of convicted criminals. Some 600 prisoners on death rows across the country had their sentences commuted to life in prison. During the five years between 1972 and 1976 the death penalty was more than crippled as a possible deterrent to murder. It was legally removed as a deterrent.

This five-year *abolishment* period offered interested states the opportunity to independently submit new death-penalty statutes to the Supreme Court for their approval on a state-by-state basis. The abolishment period ended when the Supreme Court upheld the constitutionality of statutes submitted by three states.

The process of gaining Supreme Court approval of new statutes as other states followed suit was important procedurally for the present study. States that were interested had to have the political will and the moral disposition to undergo a difficult screening process at about the same time in our criminal justice history. In other words, they all received approval under much the same circumstances, a commonality that did not exist at earlier times of choice.

Thirty-eight states eventually received approval of their death-penalty statutes and remained committed to capital punishment throughout the inhibition period (1977–2003) except for occasional lapses. These 38 will be considered the *death-penalty* states. Twelve states plus the District of Columbia (included as the 13th state for writing simplicity) did not adopt capital punishment or in a few cases relinquished the death penalty soon after their statutes were approved. These will be designated as the *no-death penalty control* states. State preference for using capital punishment as a deterrent or not remained remarkably constant over the moratorium and abolishment years. This meant that the earlier study of inhibition loss (disinhibition) between 1958 and 1976 and the later study of inhibition (between 1977 and 2003) could be conducted with much the same research grouping of states.

Creating the Research Periods in the Study

The nine-year stoppage in the possibility of an effective capital punishment system represents the linchpin period in this study of deterrence. What happened during this period provides two opportunities to examine *disinhibition* or release of willful killing. The first four years (1968–1971) involved a termination of executions. Although capital punishment statutes remained in place, no convicted criminals were put to death. This *moratorium* could only weaken capital punishment systems. The next five years followed upon the decision of the Supreme Court that the death penalty was unconstitutional; this will be designated as the *abolishment* period (1972–1976).

In order to demonstrate disinhibition, the weakening and then disappearance of capital punishment as a deterrent should be accompanied by successive increments in the murder rate and individual murder count of death-penalty states. However, any disinhibitory changes in intentional killing would require a comparison with some prior time for each state as well as with control states in way of proof. Accordingly, a period of ten years (1958–1967) before the moratorium began was designated as a *baseline* period for this comparison. Nothing major seemed to have happened in the courts during this period with respect to the death penalty. Nevertheless Vila and Morris (1997) identified a shift from social commentary on this subject to legal debate regarding its constitutionality. While none of this succeeded in disrupting capital punishment, it may well have diminished the difference between baseline deterrence effect and the moratorium disinhibition effect.

The 27 post-restoration years (1977–2003), after state statutes were allowed to be reinstituted, offered me the opportunity to look for possible inhibition effects of the death penalty. Demonstrating this effect required a decrement in the murder counts for the death-penalty states over time relative to the no-death-penalty controls. The total 27-year period was broken down into three 9-year periods for analysis. This allowed any demonstrated inhibitory effect to be more closely examined to ascertain whether the decrease was linear or curvilinear. Linear would mean that the decrease in intentional killing was fairly regular from one 9-year period to the next one. Curvilinearity would mean that a decrease was evident but irregular from one time period to the next. To observe that requires at least three points of reference.

It turned out that the inhibition effects were very slow to emerge, very much in contrast to disinhibition that appeared almost immediately in 1968. The slow pace of inhibition led me to concentrate on a comparison between the first 9-year period (1997–1985) and the third 9-year period (1995–2003) in the search for inhibition effects. The results for the middle 9-year period will be reported in the forthcoming table simply for your information.

More about the Confounded Variables

The three confounded variables that were identified in this study already have been discussed to some extent. The purpose of finding these variables was to gain a broader understanding of any differences in murder counts found between states with and without the death penalty. Logic, prior research, and common sense led me to believe that any or all of these variables could be related to how well capital punishment deterred intentional killing. If so and they were not brought into the analyses, it would be possible for the oversight to mask or otherwise distort true differences in murder counts between death-penalty and control states.

Two of these confounded variables, total state population and percentage of that total represented by minorities, were thought to be positively correlated with intentional killing; the higher the population and minority presence, the greater the killing. The third confounded variable, number of executions between 1977 and 2003, was believed to be a reflection of state commitment to its own capital punishment system. Degree of commitment could determine the state's effectiveness in deterring murder; the greater the commitment, the less the killing. Since all three confounded variables play such an important part in this study, I shall offer the reader some preliminary data from the investigation relevant to my reasoning.

State Population Variables as
Related to Intentional Killing

Here is how the analysis of total population count and minority percentage proceeded in this preliminary look at their relationship to intentional killing. They were considered conjointly as state population characteristics hypothetically related to difficulty of deterrence and, in turn, to the prevalence of murder. To test this I turned to the inhibition evidence for the critical first and last 9-year periods. The question came down to this. Were total population of the state and the minority representation in that total conjointly related to state murder rate? Hawaii and the District of Columbia were eliminated from this analysis, since neither offered the white majority required by minority percentage as a confounded variable. Two analyses were conducted: for the 1977–1985 period when the death penalty was initially restored, and for 1995–2003 when collection of data ended in this deterrence study.

The analytic procedures were simple. In the 1977–1985 analysis the average population (1980 census) of the 49 states was about 2,750,000 people, and the average minority percentage was between 10% and 11%. The two population variables were split at their mid-points and then separated into four categories: high on both, high on one and low on the other, the opposite low-high, and low on both. The 1995–2003 analysis (2000 census) followed the same procedure with an average population of 4,000,000 and average minority representation of about 16%. The average murder rate for each pairing is found in Table 1. Note that this analysis did not consider whether states had the death penalty or not.

Two conclusions are evident when you examine Table 1. In the earlier time period the combination of a higher state population and a higher state minority percentage in that population was associated with the highest murder rate; a lower count in both was associated with the lowest murder rate. When one is above the average and one is below, the murder rate

Table 1

State Population and Minority Percentage as Related to Murder Rate in the 1977-1985 and 1995-2003 Periods

	1977-1985		1995-2003	
	Number of States	Average Murder Rate	Number of States	Average Murder Rate
High SP and High MP	17	10.5	15	7.7
High SP and Low MP	8	6.7	10	4.6
Low MP and High SP	7	7.4	9	7
Low SP and MP	17	3.8	15	2.5

Note: SP = state population; MP = minority percentage

assumes an intermediate value. The second conclusion is apparent when you look in the "number of states" column; high values tend to cluster together as do low values. The predominant combinations among the states in the 1977–1985 analysis was a large population coupled with many minorities or a small population with relatively few minorities.

Moving to the 1995–2003 period in Table 1 you can see that both conclusions remain the same but perhaps not quite as striking. The data overall represent a replication of findings and satisfy the research requirement of reliability. Allow me to reiterate, then, what shall be an oft-repeated commentary on deterrence effect from this point on. Many states, the majority in fact, contend with intentional killing at opposite poles of inherent social difficulty. Some states, those with large populations and many minority residents, have to deal with the most serious social challenge to deterrence. The states at the opposite pole, those with a small population and limited minority representation within that population, confront the least serious social challenge to deterrence. It is not appropriate to question the specific deterrence value for the death penalty within a state unless you stipulate these population characteristics for that state.

Since the combination of the two population variables is going to bear some of the explanatory weight as the results of the study are interpreted, I shall report one further analysis of their relationship to intentional killing in a form that may be more readily assimilated. By turning them around, you will be able to examine the population characteristics that are related to high and low murder rate. The results will mean the same thing, of course, but you will get a different version of their relationship.

Only the 1995–2003 period was considered for this analysis as the most recent; the 1977–1985 data would have shown the same results. The murder rates for the 49 states (remember, Hawaii and the District of Columbia were not included because they did not have a white majority) were distributed from low to high and then cut at the middle value. States with lower values (mean murder rate of 3.1) had total populations averaging 2,899,000 and minority percentages with an average of 10.4%. States with higher rates (mean rate of 7.8) presented total populations averaging 8,164,000; their average minority percentage fell at 25.3%. Now you can see that when larger states with higher minority percentages or smaller states with lower minority representation are referenced as the social context in which a deterrent must exert its effect, the differences in population characteristics are substantial.

Since Table 1 is the reader's first exposure to actual murder rates collected for the study, it might be timely to comment on how low they may seem to be. Is all this fuss about deterrence worthwhile with rates that low per 100,000 people in a state? Try multiplying a murder rate of 7.4 in the most populous state reported in the 2000 census with over

32,000,000 people. That would bring the number of individual murders up to almost 2400 in a given year. That qualifies as an ominous figure.

Effectiveness of the Capital Punishment System as Related to Intentional Killing

The third confounded variable that qualified logically as a determinant of deterrence value for capital punishment was the number of executions that were actually conducted in a given state over the entire 27 year post-restoration period. This number was taken as an indicator of a philosophy of punishment of sorts relevant to the death penalty and a determinant of how effective the capital punishment system would be in a given state. The more effective the system, the stronger should be the deterrence value of the death penalty.

There are assumptions here that require confirmation by evidence. That will come in the next chapter as part of the primary analysis. At this preliminary stage I hope you will settle for reasoning that leads me to assume that number of executions in a state will influence the deterrence value of capital punishment.

Here goes. Two things seem basic to arousing fear of execution and subsequence deterrence. First, someone with an impulse to kill must be aware that the death penalty is a possibility should that person engage in willful killing. Second, even if aware of the state statutes regarding capital punishment, an individual must be convinced that the state actually exacts this penalty enough to warrant serious concern. There are complications in this reasoning. For example, the person must be able to experience fear of punishment for criminal activity to the degree most of us do. A psychopath at the extreme would not.

States that rarely exact the terms of their death-penalty statutes to the fullest by executing a murderer convicted in a capital case run the risk of limiting deterrence value. Treatment one way or another by the media represents one of the few ways that residents of a state are reminded that the death penalty exists as a punishment. Few executions mean little media attention. Aside from lack of awareness or at least uncertainty regarding commitment to the death penalty inherent in a restricted number of executions, there is the reverse problem of someone who does take note of the infrequency. Few executions. Low risk. Less fear.

Halperin's table showing number of executions performed between 1977 and 2003, compiled by state for the internet, was useful in introducing frequency of executions into the deterrence study as a confounded variable. The range in frequency for the 27-year period after the death penalty was reinstated in 1977 is almost beyond belief. States that adopted capital punishment varied in execution count from 1 to 313 according to this table. Six executions represented the number that most closely divided the death-penalty states into high-execution and low-execution groupings of about the same size. My expectation was that these execution groupings would lead to differences in state murder rates. The sheer difference in number of executions lends confidence to this expectation. The low-execution states, for example, averaged about 2 executions over 27 years. I would imagine that an execution every 13 years would not be enough to keep many residents in a state even aware that they had a capital punishment system.

My take on the paucity of executions in these low-execution states ignores the possibility that these states simply did not have very many murders that could lead to capital prosecution, proof of guilt, and the death penalty. One execution every 13 years on average requires something beyond a more benevolent society, however. Something has gone amiss in their capital punishment systems. Perhaps prosecution has been too cautious, or juries have proven reluctant to mandate the death penalty. Then there is always the possibility of a post-trial indecisiveness about execution itself.

To briefly summarize my conclusions concerning the three confounded variables in the study ahead, they all have the potential to clarify the issue of whether the existence of capital punishment statutes in a state serves to deter intentional killing. Total state population and minority percentage in that population, combined, should tell us how difficult it would be to effectively deter the act of murder. The number of executions in death-penalty states may give us a look at two levels of deterrent effectiveness. Both levels can be compared to control states as far as inhibition of intentional killing is concerned. In addition, we will have the opportunity to examine whether these two death-penalty groups with an apparently different commitment to that punishment will demonstrate divergent disinhibition effects.

Chapter 3

Results of the Study

Before we begin examining the data that will let us judge whether the death penalty has deterrent value when it comes to intentional killing, a couple of reminders are in order. The deterrence value of the death penalty will be considered in the context of confounded variables that are critical to making this judgment. Two of them are parameters of state population, total count and minority percentage in that total. These will be considered as determinants of how difficult the task of deterring murder will be in a particular state with higher numbers indicating greater difficulty.

The third confounded variable is the degree of state commitment to the capital punishment system it has adopted as evidenced by the number of times over a 27-year span (1977–2003) that a state had fully followed through on the terms of its death-penalty statutes by the execution of a convicted criminal after a capital murder case. Those with fewer executions will be referred to from this point on as the "weak death-penalty" states and those with more executions as the "strong death-penalty" states. It was proposed that more executions would enhance awareness of the death penalty and increase the perceived certainty of lethal punishment for murder.

State Total Population, Minority Percentage, and Commitment to Capital Punishment as Confounded Variables

Table 2 includes the average population counts and the average minority percentages for the three research groups that will be used in the study: the no death-penalty control group (12 states plus Washington D.C.), the weak death-penalty group (20 states), and the strong death-penalty group (18 states). Three U.S. census reports are considered in covering the entire period of study—1970, 1980, and 2000. The 1990 census was not consulted since the middle nine years of the inhibition period (1986–1994) did not prove to be particularly revealing except as an extension of the first nine years of the inhibition period. Inhibition was slow to appear.

Table 2
Average State Populations and Average Minority Percentages for the Three Research Groups and Over Three Census Reports

	Average State Population			Average Minority Percentage		
	1970	1980	2000	1970	1980	2000
No Death Penalty	2,476,000	2,819,000	2,896,000	5.0%	6.3%	9.3%
Weak Death Penalty	3,515,000	3,812,000	4,258,000	9.1%	11.2%	16.6%
Strong Death Penalty	5,547,000	6,538,000	7,987,000	16.3%	18.7%	24.3%

The Table 2 data make it evident that the three research groups differed radically in average population size and average minority percentage of that population. The states that chose not to have capital punishment were on average much smaller states in total population and lower in minority representation. At the other extreme, the states opting for the death penalty that subsequently demonstrated a stronger commitment to their systems of capital punishment had the largest population and highest minority counts by far. The states with capital punishment that seemed to show little interest in enforcing these statutes fell in between these extremes. They were closer, however, to the control states in their average populations and minority representation. The relative standing of the research groups on the confounded population variables remained quite constant from the 1970 to the 2000 census with progressive increases in both state populations and minority percentages.

Moving from the population numbers in Table 2 to their meaning, there seems little doubt in my mind that the strong death-penalty states had the most formidable challenge when it came to suppressing intentional killing. States without capital punishment had the least problem with willful killing. The weak death-penalty states fell in-between as far as being confronted with lethal violence in their populations.

Although these population differences still do not bring us to the deterrence results for the death penalty, they do confirm important social context differences for understanding these results when they are reported. In the present study the strong death-penalty states should have found it considerably more difficult than the weak death-penalty group to limit murder rate or the absolute count of intentional killings given their population parameters. People in states without capital punishment should not experience the threat of execution unless they are uninformed or confused about state law, so the reasoning stops there as far as deterrence goes. Yet the relatively low values of control-state populations and minority percentages are still important, since these values would lead you to expect only a restricted number of murders. That cannot be attributed to the effect of capital punishment, but it can help explain why they chose not to have the death penalty. The need for a strong deterrent was lacking.

Using the two population parameters and level of commitment to a death-penalty system as guides to a state's potential for intentional killing can be an elusive business. Like most conclusions from data in social science it is based on inference, hypothesis, and plain common sense. There was no direct measure of potential for social violence available for this study except the murder counts that are to be reported ahead. Yet there is a welcome confirmation in the Table 2 data that my reasoning is potentially on target regarding how we should regard deterrence effect. It is not just a matter of obtaining an arithmetic value based upon an intentional-killing count but should consider the level of violence in a society and how difficult it was achieving that value. Stipulating an effect should also take into consideration the level of deterrence that has been exerted in curbing that violence.

I will not stop there in celebrating the Table 2 results though. They also allow us to extend our reasoning to explaining how the three research groups came to coalesce for purposes of this study. As I have noted, the 13 states that chose not to adopt the death penalty would have been in the most likely position to not do so. They were faced with only a limited problem of willful killing (as signaled by low population and restricted minority representation), so their disinterest in capital punishment may have been based more on limited need for a severe disincentive as on moral objection.

The weak death-penalty states are somewhat of an enigma. Why adopt capital punishment and then seemingly not take the statutes seriously? Their intermediate status on the population parameters offers an answer. Their social problems promoting intentional killing may have been serious enough to encourage adoption of capital punishment statutes but not serious enough to ward off opposition to the death penalty. One approach to resolving the inevitable conflict would be to maintain the death penalty to satisfy supporters at one pole but limit the executions so as to not arouse moral opposition at the other pole. A middling social demand for suppression of willful killing would be at the heart of the issue.

The strong death-penalty grouping of states had the most formidable task ahead of them in suppressing intentional killing when they regained the use of capital punishment after 1977. The re-adoption and continuing commitment to the use of the death penalty as the years went by would likely reflect state need to use whatever deterrence they could muster to suppress the problems with lethal violence inherent in very large populations and relatively large minority percentages.

Disinhibition as One Requirement of a Deterrent

You will recall that full proof that the death penalty in a given state serves as a deterrent to intentional killing in that state involves two requirements—proof of disinhibition and proof of inhibition. Disinhibition would be reflected in an increase in intentional killing given less chance that the individual would be executed for committing the act. Proof of an inhibition effect requires that intentional killings would decrease given an increased probability that execution would follow committing the act.

To extend my reasoning to the confounded variables, I proposed not only that inhibition of intentional killing would increase given greater certainty that the death penalty could be imposed but that level of violence would serve as counter-active variable. Inhibition would be more difficult in states with more violent societies. Both heightened inhibition and greater counteraction should converge in the strong death-penalty states. These states feature greater commitment to their death-penalty statutes but also a more formidable problem with lethal violence that goes with greater population and minority size. This could pose a problem in showing capital punishment to be a deterrent.

Table 3 will give us our first look at evidence concerning whether capital punishment serves as a deterrent to murder by examining disinhibition of intentional killing. Does murder increase when the death penalty is first obstructed nationally and then totally abolished? Three time periods will be compared allowing conclusions to be drawn regarding the occurrence of disinhibition. The *baseline period* (1958–1967) represents the ten years prior to the legal devastation of capital punishment in the United States following several Supreme Court decisions. By and large, the baseline period offered a fairly normal span of years as far as the courts were concerned, although there was a growing recognition that the death penalty was fair game for challenge in the courts by its detractors.

The *moratorium period* (1968–1971) involved the cessation of executions, although capital punishment statutes remained on the books. Prosecutors stopped short of execution in capital cases, since they anticipated the possibility of reversal based upon several Supreme Court decisions concerning the constitutionality of the death-penalty verdict. The four years represented a time when the death penalty was weakened as a deterrent but not totally dismantled.

The *abolishment period* (1972–1976) followed upon a decision by the Supreme Court that capital punishment was unconstitutional. Those five years provide a time when the death penalty was not only diminished as a deterrent but no longer existed.

To the extent that the death penalty serves as a deterrent to intentional killing, the murder count should increase as we move from baseline to moratorium to abolishment periods. Two measures of intentional killing will be reported as promised. Murder rate will give us the number of murders per 100,000 people for a given state and year. It will allow for direct comparison of states differing in population or the same state over time as its population changes. The numbers you will see in Table 3 will be averages and very stable. These averages will be computed over states in death-penalty groupings and over years within the three disinhibition periods—baseline, moratorium, and abolishment. Individual count provides the actual number of killings in a state for a given year and allows us to gauge how much the state contributes to the national homicide problem. Again the murder counts you will see in Table 3 will be averages for the control, weak death-penalty, and strong death-penalty groups over the years within the three disinhibition periods.

Table 3

Effects of Diminishing Legal Status of the Death Penalty and Degree of Commitment to the Death Penalty Upon Disinhibition of Willful Killing

Degree of Commitment		Legal Status		
		Baseline Period (1958-1967)	Moratorium Period (1968-1971)	Abolishment Period (1972-1976)
No Death Penalty	MR	2.9	4.5	5.4
	IC	64.4	121.8	149.1
Weak Death Penalty	MR	3.8	5.6	6.8
	IC	137.4	226.1	286.4
Strong Death Penalty	MR	7.3	9.4	11.0
	IC	362.0	484.0	601.4

Note: MR = murder rate; IC = individual murder count. Both numbers represent yearly averages taken over all states in the particular death-penalty group and all years in the legal-status period being examined.

I hope the reader will excuse what may seem like digressing, but Table 3 represents the first exposure in the book to this kind of complex tabled data. I would like to walk you through a bit of it to be sure that it is clearly presented. First, how the numbers were determined and then to the interpretation. I will use the no-death-penalty control states to explain the procedure. Murder rate (MR) averages found in each legal-status time period of the table for the 13-state control group (2.9, 4.5, 5.4) are for each year of the time period. Just looking at the 2.9 figure for the baseline period, this is the average MR for each state further averaged over the 10-year period. Said another way, 2.9 per 100,000 people gives us the average rate of murder in each control state during each year preceding the demise of capital punishment.

The individual count (IC) was determined by taking the average murder rate for a state and converting it into the number of individuals it represents in light of the number of 100,000 units of population. This absolute figure provides the number of people intentionally killed during a year for a particular death-penalty group and during a particular legal-status period. Or if you prefer, the IC provides a very stable estimate of how much each group of states adds yearly to the national problem of people intentionally killing one another.

Now to interpretation of the disinhibiton results. It is not difficult to identify a disinhibition effect. The increasing trends of Table 3 data as the chances diminished that the death penalty could serve as a deterrent are apparent throughout the table. Both murder rate and individual murder count increase over the two successive periods following baseline. A conundrum presents itself though in that this effect can be noted in all three death-penalty groups including the control states that chose not to employ capital punishment. In fact, these control states demonstrated that greatest increase in murder rate from baseline. The MR increment for control states from baseline to moratorium (55.8%) and then from moratorium to abolishment (28.5%) was stronger in a percentage sense than shown by the weak or the strong death-penalty groups.

At the other extreme, the strong death-penalty states demonstrated a substantial disinhibition effect but the lowest percentage figures when it came to incremental change in intentional killing—baseline to moratorium (34.9%) and moratorium to abolishment (19.2%) in yearly rate. The weak death-penalty group assumed its customary intermediate position between control states and strong death penalty states (45.4% and 23.7%). All groups demonstrated changes suggesting disinhibition. However a puzzle exists in the order of magnitude and in why the control states should show an increase in murder at all. I did not do a good job in working this puzzle out in an earlier effort, but I am confident that I have a better explanation now (see next chapter).

The second set of numbers found in Table 3 gives us the average individual count of murders per year shown by the state groupings in each time period. This number, while correlated with murder rate, provides a clearer and more understandable picture regarding the death penalty as a deterrent of intentional killing. Diminished deterrent effectiveness leading to an upsurge in the count of individual murders is clearest in states that demonstrated a strong death penalty system. Disinhibition in high-population states with high minority percentages would be expected to result in such a surge, since they are burdened with substantial problems with lethal violence even under the strongest conditions of deterrence. Their increased numbers of intentional killings under conditions of disinhibition add significantly to the national murder toll.

Put into arithmetic terms, you can see quite graphically what the release of lethal violence did during the moratorium on executions and sequentially by the abolishment of capital punishment. Consider, especially, what happened in the strong death-penalty states during the demise of capital punishment at the extreme. The intentional killing in each state increased by almost 240 cases a year on average (to over 601) from an already high baseline of murders (362).

Inhibition as the Second Requirement of a Deterrent

The interpretive task in studying inhibition as a second requirement for judging whether capital punishment serves as a deterrent to intentional killing proved to be less complicated than was true for disinhibition, and I have not even gotten to all the complications of the disinhibition findings. That will come in the next chapter. The difference between understanding the results for the two processes is largely a conceptual one. Understanding deterrence, for me at least, is more straightforward if you think of it in terms of suppression of an act when the deterrent is present than when you consider release of the act when the deterrent is removed. Also, there were no surprises lurking in the inhibition results requiring me to dig deeper conceptually to come up with a satisfactory explanation. The disinhibition analysis did bring confirmation of this required effect, but it brought some puzzling results as well that are not likely to be considered in deterrence research.

One thing was obvious in both the inhibition and disinhibition data. Neither was an all-or-nothing process. In both analyses the results did not portray the suppressing or releasing effect on willful killing as the sole property of one research group of states. Differences in apparent disinhibition and inhibition were a matter of degree. Welcome to the world of social science!

Confounded Variables in the Inhibition Analyses

The primary analyses of inhibition will entail comparisons between the initial 9-year post-restoration period (1977–1985) and the final 9-year post-restoration period (1995–2003). These periods were chosen because they represented the earliest inhibition could begin after capital punishment was restored to constitutional favor and the latest it could be measured as the study ended. It was mentioned earlier that the middle inhibition period (1986–1994) was not subjected to close analysis because so little change in the two counts of intentional killing had occurred by that time in the total inhibition period. Murder rates for that middle period will be included in the table ahead as reference points, however, and you can see for yourself how slowly inhibition was rebuilt. Both the first and third 9-year periods made use of the most relevant United States census for state population figures—1980 and 2000, respectively.

As in the disinhibition analyses, confounded variables, state population and minority percentage, were used to examine the very important question of how dangerous the states are as far as being vulnerable to intentional killing is concerned? In other words, how difficult a task faced the state in deterring willful killing? Increased numbers for both state population and minority percentage, taken in combination, were found to be associated with a higher murder rate in a state. Increased numbers would provide a more formidable challenge to inhibition.

Looking back at the numbers in Table 2 it is clear that the major differences in the state population parameters in 1970 were between the strong death-penalty group of states and the other two research groupings. The differences that were quite clear among the research groups in 1970 became even more obvious in 1980 and 2000. State populations? Compare the *difference* in average total population for no-death penalty states and for strong death-penalty states across census years. About 3,000,000 difference in average state size between the small control states and the large strong-death-penalty states in 1970, going on a 4,000,000 difference in 1980, and over a 5,000,000 difference in average state population in 2000.

Minority percentage? The difference in 1970 between the lower average of the control states and the higher average of the strong death-penalty states was 11.3%; 12.4% in 1980; and 15.0% in 2000. The disparity between the no-death-penalty and strong death-penalty average minority percentages started large and got larger. Considering both confounded population variables, the story was the same. Both pointed to a more difficult task facing the group of states that took a strong stance on capital punishment relative to the no-death-penalty states. Death-penalty states with weak systems faced an intermediate degree of lethal violence but a level more similar to the control states.

As we move on to considering inhibition of intentional killing, we will be concerned with how great an inhibition effect was demonstrated over the first and then over the third 9-year periods. As will be no surprise, the important issues of system effectiveness and how difficult a task the states faced in suppressing intentional killing will not be ignored.

The Inhibition of Intentional Killing

Comparison in inhibition effect between the death-penalty state groups is represented in Table 4. Murder rate (MR) and individual murder count (IC) are presented for the first nine years of the 27-year post-restoration period as well as the final nine years of the study. The MR numbers are given for the middle years to give the reader a sense of pace for inhibitory change for the whole period.

Scanning the entire matrix of numbers in Table 4 reveals a decline in intentional killing from the first 9-year average to the final 9-year average for all groups. The no-death-penalty control states demonstrated the least decline in average MR (21%); the weak death-penalty states decreased their average MR more substantially (24%); strong death-penalty states showed the greatest decline in average MR (29%). Accordingly, the decrements in murder rate, measured by percentage drop and indicating inhibition, were in the predicted order given the threat of execution as a deterrent to willful killing.

Table 4
Effects of Degree of Commitment to the Death Penalty Upon Inhibition of Willful Killing

Degree of Commitment		Inhibition Period		
		1977-1985	1986-1994	1995-2003
No Death Penalty	MR	5.0	(5.0)	3.9
	IC	138.1		116.8
Weak Death Penalty	MR	6.2	(6.0)	4.8
	IC	282.4		228.6
Strong Death Penalty	MR	10.4	(9.7)	7.4
	IC	710.0		609.5

Note: MR = murder rate; IC = individual murder count. Both numbers represent averages taken over all states in the particular death-penalty group and all years in the inhibition period. The 1986-1994 period was not further analyzed.

The IC numbers where absolute count is our concern also point to a clear-cut inhibition effect for capital punishment, one that would amount to a significant reduction in the national toll. Let me take you through the numbers. Consider the control states first, and we gain a picture of what happened between the 1977–1985 span and the 1995–2003 period without the death penalty as a deterrent to murder. There was a reduction of 21.3 intentional killings as a yearly average for each state in the control group as we compare the first nine years of the post-restoration period with the last nine years. This drop in IC converts into an estimate of 2500 fewer murders in the latter period given there were 13 states and 9 years to be considered.

However, if you work this out for the weak death-penalty grouping of states, the estimate for lives spared between 1995 and 2003 by the inhibition of intentional killing reaches almost 9700. States with a strong death penalty experienced a collective reduction of more than 16,000 murders over the 18 states during the final nine years of the study when they dropped their yearly average IC by just over 100 victims.

Given these numbers, particularly for the strong death-penalty group, perhaps it would not be remiss of me to once again remind the reader that both death-penalty groups of states were working against the tide of lethal violence that would be expected in large-population/higher minority-percentage states. This requires special acknowledgement for the states with a strong death penalty. They not only demonstrated the greatest drop in murder rate in addition to the expected largest reduction in individual murder count but did so despite two ominous harbingers of willful killing in those states. They were dealing with runaway elevations in population and in minority representation.

There is one more comparison that you might find interesting given the results in Table 4. Let us look back further over the years to a comparison of murder rate for the baseline period (1958–1967) and the final period under investigation (1995–2003). That allows for a comparison of murder rates for the research groups found before Supreme Court activism altered the procedures (and effectiveness) of capital punishment and the murder rates after the 9-year hiatus and up to 27 years of attempted deterrence by reinstated death-penalty statutes.

Control states that laid no claim to capital punishment ended up the study in 1995–2003 with an average yearly MR that remained 34% above their yearly average during the relatively uneventful baseline years. States that chose to adopt capital punishment but seemed lukewarm in their commitment to its statutes did better but persisted 26% above their baseline murder rate. Given a stronger commitment to capital punishment, states were able to bring their average rate of murder down to within 1% of their earlier baseline standard. And certainly not for the last time, I would remind you that the strong death-penalty states accomplished this despite far more formidable problems with lethal violence than states in the other two groupings.

A final note in this chapter before I move on. There may be some concern that the reduction in intentional killing found in 1995–2003 could be better explained as part of a decreasing incidence of violent crime in general across the country and not as an effect specific to inhibition by capital punishment. There are two reasons why this argument can be disregarded. First, how would the contention that the decreasing murder counts were simply one aspect of a lowering incidence of violence in general explain the differences among the death-penalty groups? These differences did, after all, conform to the importance of capital punishment as a deterrent.

The second reason this argument can be ignored is that there was no reduction in nonlethal violence during the period in question. The national murder rate dropped 31% from 1972–1976 highs when the death penalty was abolished to the final period in the study. During the same period, cases involving the most serious forms of nonlethal violence (forcible rape, robbery, aggravated assault) rose 30% at the national level. The *decrease* in intentional killing is readily attributable in important measure to the restoration of the death penalty, especially in a committed way. Intentional killing even shows an inhibition effect relative to control states when commitment to the death penalty seems lacking. At the same time, nonlethal violence demonstrated an *increase* nationwide.

Chapter 4

What to Make of the Results

I believe the results of the deterrence study that we have considered in this book call for only one conclusion. The death penalty, almost exclusively reserved for the ultimate crime of murder under especially egregious conditions, serves a useful function in the American society by saving lives of people who do not deserve to die. The evidence suggests that having this severe punishment as a possible consequence for the crime of intentionally killing another person reduces the likelihood that people will act on the impulse to murder. The fear of execution is proposed as the deterrent to action with reduction of this fear by restraint of the act serving to reinforce the choice.

Having capital punishment statutes in place is not all that a state needs to do in order to best ameliorate the problem of intentional killing. The results also made it clear that death-penalty states must allow the capital punishment system to satisfy its statutes before the threat of execution can be most effective as a deterrent to murder. Partitioning the death-penalty states by number of executions over a 27-year period revealed that the half that rarely executed a prisoner convicted of a capital crime (about 1 every 13 years on average) were less able to inhibit willful killing. They were more successful than states without the death penalty, however. States that executed more, sometimes many more, had a better deterrence record. I would explain this difference in communication terms laced with perception. People in a state need to know that it has capital punishment and, furthermore, that the state has a commitment to enforcing its statutes. These are a matter of communication. Awareness of both (perception) would contribute to the fear of acting on homicidal impulse for the individual.

Of course, there may be other ways of interpreting the wide variance in number of executions in death-penalty states. For example, it could be reasoned that it is not the limited number of executions that is key to understanding these differences but rather the small number of capital murder cases in a state and the corresponding few criminals sentenced to be executed. Said another way, the "weak death-penalty" states (my term) could have satisfied the statutes governing execution as strictly as other states but may have prosecuted only a very limited number of cases that allowed for the death penalty.

I do not have access to the information that would help make the distinction between weak enforcement of capital punishment statutes by the state and a rare need to activate the statutes. In my mind it makes no difference anyway. Whether a state with capital punishment sends more prisoners to death row who languish there awaiting execution or send very few to await execution in the expected course of time, the implication remains the same. There is laxity somewhere in the system whether it is in the limited prosecution of capital murder or in the halting completion of the terms of capital conviction. Either way there is likely to be limited awareness of the death penalty in the state. The result? Less deterrence value.

While a bit of a stretch, there is yet another interpretation of the nearly absent number of executions. Some states may be populated by people who rarely engage in anything so violent as capital murder. That ranks right up there with a belief in Santa Claus and Mary Poppins.

It is worth repeating that the weak death-penalty states did demonstrate a deterrence effect during the inhibition analysis relative to the no-death-penalty control states. The presence of even a pallid version of capital punishment is still preferable to depending on incarceration alone to inhibit intentional killing. It was only by comparison with a more involved version of capital punishment, one that resulted in many more executions, that weak death-penalty states demonstrated the limitations of poorer commitment. Strong death-penalty states produced not only a higher inhibition of intentional killing but did so despite a far more formidable challenge in what were especially violent states.

The introduction of confounded variables into the investigation of deterrence also helped to explain some things about capital punishment that more often than not go unexplained, probably unrecognized. We have just considered strength of the capital punishment system as one such variable that is usually ignored in the discussion of its value as a deterrent. First law of social dynamics: If something has an intended psychological effect, then increasing its strength will probably increase its intended effect.

Two state population parameters, total population and minority percentage, represented the other two confounded variables. Like strength of the capital punishment system they proved invaluable in explicating the deterrence results. Their relevance to murder rate and individual count of murders has already received emphasis in understanding the true deterrence value of a capital punishment system. If a deterrent has produced its inhibition effects in a state with a large population and substantial minority percentage, its deterrence value should be considered greater than indicated. Soon I will make important use of these confounded population variables in offering an explanation of the reverse order of disinhibition effects observed during the moratorium and abolishment years.

Adding even more to their explanatory value, these two population variables helped clarify why some states remain aloof from capital punishment and the remaining states vary in their willingness to implement the terms of the death-penalty statutes. The fact is that the no-death-penalty control states are those that least need a serious deterrent to murder. They are primarily small-population states with only a limited number of people from minority groups. Taken together these factors lend themselves to low murder counts and the absence of a compelling reason for extraordinary deterrence measures. Much the same conclusion can be reached for the weak death-penalty states that adopt capital punishment but do not make effective use of its deterrence effect.

This is all repetition in order to make a point. Falling back on moral reasoning to avoid or underutilize capital punishment is probably not necessary. A moral rationale would not be required if these states simply promulgated the statistics showing murder rate and individual murder count were not so high as to make the death penalty essential as a deterrent. Come to think of it, that would imply that the savings in lives that would probably follow adopting capital punishment would not be worth the stigma of executing prisoners convicted of capital murder. I would like to see that choice put to a vote.

There was one set of results that qualified as puzzling in light of the conclusion that the death penalty represents a deterrent to murder. You may recall that there was a release of intentional killing in death-penalty states following cessation of executions between 1968 and 1971. This was followed by further escalation between 1972 and 1976 when the Supreme Court ruled capital punishment unconstitutional. This upsurge of murder following the demise of capital punishment in the United States allowed us to examine disinhibition, one of the two requirements that define deterrence. Limiting or removing a true deterrent is shown by an increase in willful killing (disinhibition); strengthening a true deterrent is shown by a decrease in willful killing (inhibition).

What, then, was the conundrum posed by the disinhibition results? There were three research groups of states distinguished by their degree of commitment to capital punishment. A *control group* had no interest in capital punishment and did not make use of it. A *weak death-penalty group* had enough interest to adopt it but did not show much commitment to its use when it did. A *strong death-penalty group* with substantial interest not only adopted it but demonstrated a more serious interest in satisfying its statutes.

Given these three differing philosophies of punishment it might be expected that the strong death-penalty group would show the largest disinhibition effect, especially in light of the more violent societies within these large-population/high-minority-percentage states that would leave them with the greatest need to suppress intentional killing. States without a death-penalty and with the least violent societies should show the smallest disinhibition effect, since there was no lost deterrent. The disinhibition of the weak death-penalty states should fall in between these extremes. While all research groups displayed an upsurge in intentional killing, the order of magnitude for those groups ran opposite to expectation. Why would states with the greatest need for the death penalty as a deterrent and the greatest commitment to that form of punishment show the least upsurge of willful killing? Furthermore, why would another group of states with no death penalty and more benign societies experience the greatest upsurge in intentional killing?

I am now convinced that a more complex explanation is required than I offered in 2006. For one thing, I believe that two psychological processes are required to explain the disinhibition results for the death-penalty groups, not one. For another, I now believe that different explanations for the results are required for the death-penalty and control states.

First, let us consider the disinhibition effect for the death-penalty states, weak and strong. There are two psychological processes that would have been activated when the death penalty was nullified in states that place some or much value on its role as a deterrent. *Disinhibition* has received our repeated attention to this point. *Extinction* requires an explanation.

Extinction is a common enough word in our language and among its meanings is to extinguish or cause to die out. Back in the heyday of learning theory in psychology and the giants at the time—Clark Hull, Kenneth Spence, Neal Miller—extinction assumed an important role in explaining the disappearance of behavior once it had been learned. My early years as a graduate student at the University of Iowa gave me a passing familiarity with learning theory and a great deal of respect. So much for personal trivia, but at least that helps explain my inclusion, if belated, of extinction in my explanation. This will be kept as basic as possible.

Extinction of behavior, after rats had learned to press a bar that released a food pellet, occurred when the equipment no longer delivered a pellet. Extinction would take longer in some cases than in others depending, among other things, upon the strength of the habit. That, in turn, depended upon how many times the animal has been rewarded for pressing the bar when a pellet was delivered. Since rats cannot talk, the last I heard, bar-pressing was used as a behavioral substitute for what the researcher was really after: the strength of the expectation of food that had been initiated and reinforced by the delivery of pellets. Rats expected food, and this expectation extinguished (as did bar-pressing) when it was not reinforced. Humans are more complicated but the principle remains the same. Expectations extinguish when not reinforced. The stronger the expectation, the slower the extinction.

During the 1968–1976 time-span the expectations of people in the death-penalty states associated with the presence of capital punishment would not be reinforced by the reality of events. Yet expectations would persist at some level, especially in the strong death-penalty states where they have been more forcefully and frequently reinforced. Extinction need not involve denial of the moratorium on executions or of the Supreme Court ruling on constitutionality. Persistence of expectations would not have to exceed the assumption that executions would soon be reinstated or that constitutionality of capital punishment would soon be reaffirmed. Most importantly, fear of execution could still be elicited at least to some degree should a homicidal impulse occur. The persisting expectations that execution remained a risk would not be enough to prevent disinhibition, but they could very well diminish a disinhibitory effect in states that had been exposed to the death penalty as a deterrent.

People in strong death-penalty states would be the most exposed to information regarding their capital punishment systems and the most conversant with the serious commitment of their states to those systems. The expectations regarding the death penalty that persist because they are more resistant to extinction would work against the effects of disinhibition. I recognize that this rationale for why the strong death-penalty states displayed only a 35%, then 19%, increase in intentional killing during the moratorium, then abolishment, periods is not a simple one. Human learning is often a complicated matter. That two interactive processes, disinhibition and extinction, are in play would not be unusual.

This two-process rationale finds some collaboration from the weak death-penalty states in the higher murder-rate increases they experienced during the demise of capital punishment. Everything I proposed about extinction for the states with a strong death penalty would hold for the states with weak systems except extinction should be more rapid and complete and disinhibition less restricted. The higher 45% and 24% increases in murder rate for these states are consistent with more rapid and complete extinction of death penalty expectations and less opposition to disinhibition.

The third research group of states had no demonstrated interest in the death penalty as shown by their reluctance to adopt this form of punishment over the years. These states provided the most puzzling response of all to the 1968–1976 national decline and fall of capital punishment. No death penalty on the books and no commitment to a philosophy of punishment that takes a life for a life taken, yet their average increases in murder rate leads the way when capital punishment erodes during the disinhibition years. This rate rose 56% from baseline to moratorium and 28% more during the abolishment period. Of course, these were the low murder-rate states to begin with, and it did not take an epidemic increase of murder to reach these high percentages. Still, why did these states show disinhibition at all when they demonstrated so little reliance on capital punishment as a deterrent to intentional killing?

One possibility, a version of what I proposed before, is that the Supreme Court's legal distaste for the death penalty became evident when one decision after another finally limited litigation of a capital offense. This became even more evident in the decision that the death penalty itself was unconstitutional. These Supreme Court rulings could have fostered a conclusion that may or may not have been intended. Capital punishment could not be called for even when a murder occurs under the most heinous and inhumane circumstances possible. The message here, at least for people who have a glitch in their socialization, is that intentionally killing someone is "bad but not that bad"—certainly not bad enough to warrant execution. Whether this implication would be sufficient to release homicidal behavior to some small extent under normal social conditions is possible but open to debate.

Yet the years under consideration were not normal. Between 1968 and 1976 the country was still reeling from the repercussions of a war in Vietnam in which the government asked our military to take lives and lose lives for debatable reasons. Furthermore, the experience ended in an embarrassing defeat. What a time to declare that state-government executions deprived American criminals of their constitutional rights! It might be enough to anger people and tip the scales on homicidal restraint. And keep in mind that people in the no-death-penalty states should not be undergoing extinction of expectations from a period in which capital punishment was in place. An increase in lethal violence would not be counteracted by lingering expectations from a prior death-penalty system. Even a small increase in intentional killing would be enough in these low murder-rate states to affect the percentage increase that defined disinhibition.

I shall end what has been a lengthy discussion of the disinhibition results by summarizing what was clearly found rather than becoming further embroiled in the conundrum of the reversed percentage increases in the three research groups. Disinhibition, one of the requirements of a deterrent, was apparent in the increased numbers of individual murders that followed the demise of capital punishment. It also could be inferred from the murder-rate results given the importance of the extinction process that would oppose disinhibition. All of the disinhibition results point to the importance of a strong death-penalty system in states with more formidable problems of intentional killing. Even a weak system suffers when deterrence is lost and disinhibition effects occur even though they result from less violent social conditions. No-death-penalty states show the least violence but are still vulnerable to surges of willful killing unrelated to the loss of capital punishment as a deterrent.

The inhibition analysis was far more straightforward for a couple of reasons. One has to do with the fact that the inhibition effect, the second requirement of a deterrent, is more closely aligned with the common meaning of the term—something that suppresses. It also readily accommodates the fear and avoidance tandem that has been proposed as the mechanism that allows a deterrent to suppress an impulse to kill another person.

Another reason why the inhibition analysis was less of a theoretical challenge is that the results fell in line with theory and common sense. For capital punishment to qualify as a deterrent to intentional killing, the inhibition results had to demonstrate two things. Actually, the data had to show the first and the second would provide icing-on-the-cake as far as proof was concerned.

In order to infer inhibitory qualities for the death penalty it was first necessary to find that states with the strongest capital punishment systems would demonstrate the greatest decrease in willful killing over the 27 years that average numbers of annual homicides were followed. This was found. States with death-penalty systems that were weaker by execution count should have a less impressive record of suppressing intentional killing than states more committed to their death-penalty statutes. This was found as well. If this differentiation of states by strength of capital punishment systems as a deterrent has ever been made before in deterrence research, I certainly have not come across it.

Control states that reject the death penalty would be expected to experience the least inhibition of intentional killing to complete the minimum requirement for proof that the presence of capital punishment is a deterrent. Control states were able to bring the amount of lethal violence down over the inhibition period but lagged behind both death-penalty groups to a considerable extent.

The "icing-on-the-cake" for the inhibition results will surprise nobody who has read the book to this point. I have called it continually to your attention. The states differed widely on two population parameters—total state population and the percentage of that total constituted by minorities. Both parameters considered together were related to murder rate: States higher in both presented the highest rate, those lower in both had the lowest rate, and the two high-low combinations were intermediate in the rate of murder.

The point that has frequently been made is that the states with the highest population parameters by far were those that maintained the strongest capital punishment systems. This means that they should be confronted with the most challenging murder rates, and this was confirmed by actual rate figures. It also means that the most effective inhibition of intentional killing shown by these states was accomplished despite the very high level of lethal violence with which they had to contend. They demonstrated the greatest deterrence to intentional killing despite the most formidable obstacle to doing so—a more violent society. They brought this about by taking their own death-penalty statutes seriously.

Even the states that did not seem that invested in their capital punishment systems made headway, less to be sure, in bringing murder rate down over the 27-year inhibition period. That they could do this, however, was in part attributable to a less challenging set of violence problems than were encountered by their strong death-penalty counterparts.

The control states provided results that are interesting for two reasons. They round out the capital punishment triad by showing the poorest record of inhibition over the 27 years and the least ability to return their murder rates down to the levels found in the pre-moratorium baseline years. They fell behind the inhibition levels of the death-penalty states despite having the least problems with lethal violence as evidenced by their population parameters and actual murder rates.

On the other hand, the fact that the control states did bring their murder rates down as far as they did without using capital punishment as a deterrent makes it clear that there are other ways to inhibit willful killing. If it remains socially or politically repugnant to use fear of execution as a means of restraint, then it becomes especially important to understand what these alternative approaches are. The no-death-penalty states must consider, however, that there is a likely possibility that adding capital punishment and committing to its statutes stands a good chance of improving the inhibition of intentional killing.

Chapter 5

Where Do We Go From Here?

The admittedly comical answer to the question raised by the title of this chapter might well be "nowhere." Dealing with the future of capital punishment in this country, like many other countries where it has lost favor, too readily succumbs to moral sophistry. Social pragmatism that requires laws to benefit the widest swath of a society becomes buried because information is lacking. Besides, moral belief is difficult to sway. It seems to me that to do so more often than not requires proof that the moral conviction is wrong-headed without reciprocal responsibility of proving that the conviction has merit.

It is only fair to point out (before someone else does) that it could be argued that if a moral conclusion is your own and does not affect anyone else, there should be little need to question its value. Perhaps morality can remain a private concern without any impact upon others, but I doubt it. There is just too great a need to recruit others to our points-of-view or to act upon personal moral codes in relating to others for private convictions to remain private.

The ironic thing in the death-penalty controversy, however, is that the opposition to taking a life involved in state-sanctioned execution is not really central to the disagreement. Rather, the importance of who gets killed and whether there is a justifiable purpose for doing so remains at the heart of the matter. If the death penalty is a deterrent to intentional killing, and there seems to be no other way to read the evidence, then opposing capital punishment on moral grounds demonstrates willingness to trade lives. Unfortunately for the moral opposition, the trade involves an exchange of many innocent victims for each life taken by the death penalty. And these are criminals found guilty of outrageous murders by trial who have exhausted guaranteed appeals of this conviction.

Scientific evidence of deterrence is the worst enemy of those whose judgment leads them to oppose the death penalty. It casts their argument against killing other humans in a very bad light, since they are, in effect, willing to tolerate the loss of many victim lives by subverting deterrence to prevent execution of the comparatively few people who claimed victim lives in ways that degrade social order.

I find it very hard to believe that there is anything sinister going on among those who oppose the death penalty anymore than I believe that favoring capital punishment requires an apology. As I said earlier in the book, the main problem with these positions is that neither emphasizes the correct reason why we should have this or any form of extreme punishment—deterrence of intentional killing. So many seem to have bought into the pervasive conclusion that capital punishment does not deter lethal violence that it simply is ignored as a critical factor in the controversy—actually, *the* critical factor.

What I find most regrettable about this situation is that social scientists seem to have been partially responsible for the current lack of clarity in the value of the death penalty. I have commented on a few of the dubious methodologies used to study deterrence and feel no need to comment further along those lines. What I will say though, as a more general observation, is that many social scientists have contributed to a deterrence literature built on negative results, the failure to find a deterrence effect. I am sure that these researchers would insist that this follows from the absence of a deterrence effect to be found. For the sake of the reader who is not a researcher, however, let me add that negative results, the failure to find anything, are not hard to come by. Devise a poor study and you very probably will get no results worth remembering. There used to be a problem publishing a negative study when I was a part of the "publish or perish" set, but the emotional appeal of trashing the death penalty seems to have been exempt from this policy.

The Life-Without-Parole Alternative

One issue that may face those who oppose the death penalty is what, if anything, will be the standard replacement if their quest for abolishment is to continue? Even if an oppositionist were to admit that capital punishment does have some deterrence value, it could be contended that a substitute exists that is just as effective, even more so, but far more humane. In fact, that is just what is happening in our system of criminal justice. Life-without-parole (LWP) sentencing has emerged as an alternative in most if not all states. Convicted criminals who receive this sentence must remain incarcerated the remainder of their lives. No time off for good behavior. No parole. No release at the end of the prisoner's sentence.

What the availability of the LWP sentence for heinous violence means is that juries that are reluctant to impose a death sentence in the penalty phase of a capital trial or prosecutors who are hesitant to pursue the death penalty have a ready replacement available. No need to take a human life by execution when you can incarcerate criminals for the remainder of their lives. It is more humane and promises the permanent separation of a dangerous criminal from society as a benefit just as the death penalty does.

Keep in mind that this rationale for substituting LWP for capital punishment misses an important point. What about deterrence of willful killing? Those of us who believe that deterrence of future crime holds the highest priority in dispensing criminal justice would raise the question of whether

LWP will have the same deterrence value as capital punishment? Of course, if you assume that the death penalty has no deterrence value, this becomes a nonissue. It is difficult to be any less effective as a deterrent than be totally without merit. If, however, the evidence from this study is at all persuasive, some advocate in the LWP camp owes us convincing empirical evidence that demonstrates that the *threat* of mandatory lifetime incarceration would act as a serious deterrent to intentional killing.

I am not suggesting yet another poll that asks the "person in the street" to choose between capital punishment and LWP as a more likely deterrent to murder. The question of choice between these harsh forms of punishment is far too abstract and far too remote from possibility for the response to such a poll question to mean very much. If anybody cares, my response to such a poll query would certainly be the death penalty as more fear-provoking. There would be some who might actually believe that the lifetime loss of personal freedom would be a penalty worse than death. However, that is the kind of choice you might expect if you were responding to a poll without the remotest chance of being put to death. To my taste, LWP offers a guarantee of free room and board for the rest of my life, clothed and medically tended without charge, with ample time for reading. This appeals to me far more than being dead.

If a book on a somber topic like the death penalty strikes you as an unusual place for attempts at levity, allow me to apologize. Nevertheless, I am quite serious about deterrence value as the basis for choice. What we have in the increased popularity of the LWP verdict is an encroaching legal punishment that can assuage the moral sensibilities of those caught up in the criminal justice system. It is more humane to lock someone up and throw away the key following conviction for a homicide than to execute that person. Of course it is! Whether doing so can qualify as an effective way of deterring willful killing and sparing people who would otherwise be victims remains an unanswered question.

In a very real sense the current usage of the LWP sentence mirrors the way that the not-guilty-by-reason-of-insanity (NGRI) verdict found some popularity several decades ago in this country. I am not sure just how much this verdict is still used, since it was supplanted by another legal verdict, guilty-but-mentally-ill, which involved some imprisonment but the promise of treatment while there. The NGRI verdict gained momentum from Supreme Court decisions in the 1980s which protected the insane and severely mentally retarded from execution for their actions. An NGRI verdict cleared the defendant from responsibility for an act that otherwise would be considered a crime. There was a hitch to be sure. The defendant in an NGRI trial, cleared of having committed a crime, still had to stay confined in a mental hospital until given clearance for release by medical staff. Still, they were not to be considered criminals. John Hinckley, who received an NGRI verdict in 1982 after he attempted to assassinate Ronald Reagan, still has a mental hospital for a return address as far as I know.

The NGRI judgment by a jury was an attempt to do the humane thing for the mentally handicapped, but there were reasons for finding this legal outcome to be troubling. For one thing, a crime had been committed, but nobody was being held accountable. Among the extremists on the matter were those who felt that the mentally ill were being given *carte blanche* to perform what would be considered grievous crimes in the mentally normal person (like shooting a sitting president).

Taking a less emotional tone but finding some support for concern over personal responsibility in NGRI trials, a study (Heilbrun & Heilbrun, 1989) collected two samples of incarcerated men—one from mental hospitals in Florida and the other from prisons in Georgia. The mental hospital sample had performed a violent act (not necessarily murder) but received an NGRI verdict in court. The prisoners had been convicted of some type of criminal violence that matched the array of violent acts performed by the mental patients. These two samples were compared on an index of criminal dangerousness that had nothing to do with the violence in which they had engaged. This index had been previously validated as a violence measure. The higher the index, the greater the risk of serious violence. The results of the Heilbrun and Heilbrun study revealed that the NGRI patients were more dangerous by index than the ordinary violent criminals who were held responsible for their crimes. As it turned out, a predisposition to violence resided in the character of the mental patients and remained just as viable an explanation for their acts as mental disability. The question remained. Where does the responsibility that resides in an individual's personal character end and the allowances made for mental impairment begin?

The example of the NGRI verdict illustrates how a modification in criminal justice procedures that represents an effort to extend more humane treatment to violent criminals overlooked vital aspects of adjudication, especially personal responsibility for the criminal act. Relevance of the NGRI judicial experiment to the current emergence of life without parole as a more humane punishment seems clear. Many might hope that LWP would supplant the death penalty. It now seems to be the jury's alternative to execution in a capital trial, yet this has happened without examining its deterrent value to the best of my knowledge. As the alternative sentence in the type of cases found in capital prosecutions, whatever the verdict, the LWP experiment in compassion needs a lot of attention as far as deterrence of future intentional killing is concerned.

I will provide a head start from the data made available by the Death Penalty Information Center and the results of my deterrence study in assessing the deterrence value of the life-without-parole verdict. We are told that every state in the country plus the District of Columbia had adopted an LWP punishment by 2005 except Alaska and New Mexico. That means that by the end of the deterrence study (2003) it seems likely that these adoptions were largely in place. Accordingly, the inhibition results from the 1977–2003 period can tell us a little bit about LWP deterrence effects.

The control states with no death penalty but LWP statutes largely in place lagged well behind the death-penalty states, weak and strong, in the inhibition of intentional killing. They also failed to return their murder rate to baseline level by the greatest margin. That does not encourage us to believe that LWP serves as much of a deterrent. The possible effect of LWP in suppressing murder as an added deterrent is totally confounded with the effect of capital punishment in both death-penalty groups. Given the results in the control states, does anybody want to back LWP as the critical deterrent to intentional killing in states with capital punishment?

Issues Relating to the Death Penalty

As might be expected, several issues relating to capital punishment have been raised over the years besides the morality of execution and the contention that it has no deterrence effect as far as intentional killing is concerned. Some of these issues dissipate if it is acknowledged that the death penalty serves as a deterrent to intentional killing, at least according to the study we have considered at length in this book. There is at least one issue that is not readily dispelled whatever the verdict on deterrence may be. We will consider it first.

The Issue of Irreversible Error

Police investigations and courtroom procedures are vulnerable to error no matter how carefully the police and criminal justice representatives labor to establish the guilt or innocence of a suspected criminal. Mistakes are made in interpreting evidence, eyewitness accounts can be flawed, people recant their versions of the crime. Vulnerability to error is found at all levels of criminal justice, although it is a special problem in a capital case. If an innocent prisoner is executed, the error cannot be rectified as far as the executed person is concerned. It is an irreversible error.

Mistakes made in the course of establishing guilt of those accused of lesser crimes can be corrected. The living prisoners can be released from prison and even compensated to some extent for erroneous conviction and incarceration. There are irreversible errors made at less serious levels of crime as well. Sometimes there is just no evidence available to prove the innocence of a prisoner who has been wrongfully convicted or no one to search for extant evidence.

One reason why irreversible errors in capital cases may not present as serious a problem as death-penalty detractors would like to convey is the fact that prisoners sentenced to execution are confined on death row for such a protracted period before the sentence is consummated. While I have no statistics on this observation, periods of over 30 years on death row have been noted. Some of this delay is legislated for appeals. The point to be made here is that the longer someone is held on death row, the greater the opportunity for an error to be corrected. The odds may not be great in any given case, but an error is potentially reversible for all.

Another consideration relevant to the problem of irreversible errors when the death penalty is at stake is that trial procedures could be revised in a capital case so that the likelihood of an error in the verdict would be reduced. The change would not be complicated assuming the state legal systems would allow some alteration in what I understand to be standard practice in the way jurors reach decisions regarding guilt.

The change would go like this. Rather than deciding between guilty or not guilty using the familiar standard of judgment, have two standards of certainty available in capital cases. It makes little difference how the two degrees of certainty were phrased as long as instructions to the jury clearly communicated the difference. The current standard of guilt, "beyond a reasonable doubt," has a poetic ring, but it remains ambiguous enough to allow for some uncertainty. This suggested change is based on the assumption that most jurors reach a decision regarding guilt in a capital case with enough play in their judgment to allow for levels of certainty to be possible. We are used to specifying that we are "pretty certain" about some things and "very certain" about other things. Why not in capital trials? The higher standard of certainty could result in a penalty phase and the lower standard in a lesser sentence that does not allow for the death penalty. A "not guilty" verdict would retain its current meaning.

Providing a choice of three verdicts to jurors in a death-penalty trial may strike the reader as flirting with the limits of subjective judgment (for that is what jurors must depend upon). You might ask whether ordinary people, anyone for that matter, can really distinguish between "beyond a reasonable doubt" and "absolute certainty" as standards of guilt without confusion? Well, we are already asking jurors to decipher the meaning of "beyond a reasonable doubt" which assumes that the juror is capable of taking each piece of relevant evidence, analyze whether that piece of evidence is in any way fallible, and somehow integrate only the infallible pieces into a weighted summary opinion that is beyond challenge. That leaves a lot of room for levels of certainty.

Jurors in a capital case are also asked to subjectively weigh factors in the penalty phase following a guilty verdict. This may mitigate or aggravate the severity of the crime. Again the death penalty will hang in the balance. This judgment may be even more difficult than required for deciding upon the defendant's guilt in the trial. Given what we currently ask of jurors in a capital trial as far as cognitive skill goes, it does not seem too much to expose them to two levels of certainty in reaching the initial judgment regarding guilt.

Given this one recommended change, the availability of two levels of certainty in establishing guilt, it is hard to see why the problem of irreversible error would not be diminished in capital cases. If anything, the problem could become one of failing to identify enough of the criminals who deserve execution.

The Issue of Excessive Cost

It has been contended that capital punishment should be eliminated because of its excessive expense. You can run into this criticism in the news media occasionally, and it may even be accompanied by what appear to be sizable figures that ostensibly could be spent to meet more useful needs of the criminal justice systems. I have encountered the excessive-cost lament in two principal areas of expenditure—the cost of a capital trial and the cost of incarcerating a prisoner who has been sentence to death. It is difficult to verify these costs without being an accountant given access to the appropriate records. At least though we can examine the reasons offered for the excessive expense of capital punishment.

The Cost of a Capital Trial

Although I have never seen an actual breakdown of the costs associated with a capital trial, it comes as no surprise to me that trials in which the prosecution is seeking the death penalty for the alleged crime are more costly in time and money than ordinary trials. The legal system, aware that the defendant's life is at stake, seems to go to extraordinary lengths to allow for a competent defense. Of course, it is rarely a level playing field in terms of lawyers, expert witnesses, investigative staff, and other trial requisites. Since inadequate legal resources for the defendant may result in a mistrial, the courts are likely to be attentive to this issue.

I can share an anecdote with you that dramatizes the potential economic burden of a capital trial. Some 2–3 years ago as my wife and I were moving from Georgia to another state, a capital trial was underway in Atlanta. The defendant was accused of murdering two government employees who were in the course of performing their assigned duties—multiple violations of capital punishment statutes. The man had broken out of his jail cell, killed a guard, and subsequently murdered a judge in the courthouse. The crimes were witnessed by several people. Prosecution appeared to be a straightforward matter when the prisoner was brought to trial seeking the death penalty.

The state attorney-general assumed the lead-prosecutor role and added several lawyers to his team, extra insurance that nothing could go wrong in what seemed to be an "open-and-shut" case. But it did. The next-to-last thing I remember hearing about this case was that the defense insisted that the team representing the prisoner had the right to as many lawyers as the prosecution. The court agreed. The last thing I heard was that the fund used to finance the defense of indigent defendants without money was almost depleted. There was some question about how this was going to be resolved. What may have been a ploy of the defense in a hopeless case seemed to be working at state expense.

Leaving the realm of illustrative anecdote and returning to more relevant commentary on capital-trial economics, do we not have a conflict in concerns among those who oppose the death penalty? On the one hand, there are those who criticize capital punishment because there is a danger of irreversible error in a handful of cases. A way was suggested to diminish this problem. Improve the certainty of jurors in their own judgments regarding guilt before a verdict could move the proceedings into a penalty phase.

On the other hand, some choose to criticize capital punishment because the trials are overelaborate and costly. These critics, of course, would like to point to burgeoning teams of lawyers or useless testimony from expert witnesses that contradict one another. But my own anecdote aside, it would seem fairer to believe that capital trials are costly in the main because both sides are more cautious in presenting the kind and amount of information that may influence the jury.

Okay. One set of critics lament the possibility of making a
mistake in the course of a capital trial that could cost the life of
an innocent prisoner. A more elaborate (and expensive) judicial proceeding would be in order. Another set of critics de-
nounce the expense of a capital trial that would be required
for a longer and more vigorous inquiry into the prisoner's
responsibilities for the capital crime. It is difficult to view these
two criticisms as other than antagonistic. Perhaps critics of
the death penalty should talk to one another more.

The Cost of Incarceration

The second target of those who criticize capital punishment
on economic grounds is the high cost of incarcerating those
who are sentenced to be executed. Mentioned in this context
are the expenses incurred because of solitary confinement,
special guards as a security safeguard, and the lengthy period
many are held as their appeals are processed and political
issues are resolved. It may seem tactless to point out that death-
row procedures undoubtedly could be modified at curtailed
cost without endangering security or depriving sentenced prisoners ample opportunity for appeal. The length of time spent
on death row, which may represent the major excessive cost,
represents a rather strange choice for the critics of the death
penalty. Those concerned about financial matters should bear
in mind that time is the ally of belated evidence that can reduce irreversible error—recanted testimony, DNA evidence,
and the like. Being too harsh in criticizing the length of time
allowed to await execution can put the critic of capital punishment on the wrong side of the debate.

The main problem I have with length of incarceration before execution as a concern for those opposing the death penalty on economic grounds is that it represents yet another gap
in logical reasoning. What would they expect to fill the void if
the death penalty were abolished as the punishment for the
most serious types of willful killing? The current alternative

sentence in capital trials is life in prison without the possibility of parole (LWP). That would almost certainly be the choice of replacement for about everyone who opposes the death penalty. It satisfies their need for a more humane choice by not requiring the state to take a life but offers what they may presume to be equivalent justice in way of punishment.

If LWP is to be considered as the sentence of choice to replace capital punishment for those convicted of the worst crimes of lethal violence, several questions become relevant. Would the convicted murderers receive the same post-trial type of incarceration as had been required for those awaiting execution? The dangerousness of the criminals who perpetrate the most heinous violent crimes would be no less, so it might prove difficult explaining more relaxed security than before. That was one of the costly items for prisoners on death row. How about the length of time that the convicted criminals are going to be incarcerated? You cannot be held in prison longer than a lifetime without parole. What about appeals that are said to be costly? Are you going to curtail the right of appeal to prisoners who are facing the most severe punishment possible—a lifetime in prison? Not with the American Civil Liberties Union looking over your shoulder.

The long and the short of it is that the economic drain of maintaining a capital punishment system is likely to be readily matched by the cost of LWP sentencing that replaces it.

This is personal speculation but the substitution of LWP for capital punishment may well be an even greater economic albatross than that. I do not believe that the emerging LWP sentence has come close to generating its inherent costs. That lies ahead as the population of criminals in our country receiving this sentence accumulates and ages. These criminals are going to be imprisoned until the day that they die unless state government relents and makes "life without parole" a conditional rather than an absolute sentence. If this happened, if "LWP lite" were created so that parole became possible, the threat created by this sentence would be even less than it is now. Keep in mind in this regard that LWP has not been shown to come close to matching the deterrence value of the death penalty to begin with.

Returning to the potential expenses of LWP, as the disabilities of age appear the criminals receiving this sentence will have to be cared for medically and psychologically. Eventually many will have to be assisted in performing even the simplest requirements of life. The tax-payer is not going to rejoice over paying the added costs of a new concept in incarceration: the prison/nursing home. This seems especially true since the recipients of lifetime care would have canceled any obligations owed them by society with their excesses of violence.

The Issue of Biased Sentencing

It is not surprising that there have been pockets of concern about fairness of adjudication when the legal decision is as serious as the death penalty. Bias in this context would mean that a judgment is influenced one way or another by some attribute of the accused criminal that is not relevant to the issue of guilt or innocence. Bias could infiltrate criminal justice decisions in a capital case anywhere along the line: in police investigation of the case, in the choice of whether to pursue a capital prosecution, in the trial phase establishing responsibility for the crime, or in the penalty phase when execution becomes a possible choice of the jury. We will consider two possible sources of bias among many, race and gender.

Despite the ease of assuming that bias has contributed to some decisions among the vast number reached within our criminal justice systems, it is difficult to prove. There are two reasons for this that I can see. For one, different opinions frequently exist regarding whether something is relevant or is a matter of bias and not relevant. What may be considered bias by some may seem relevant to crime and punishment by others. In considering whether a woman should be convicted of a capital crime in our country, for example, what importance should be assigned to remnants of male chivalry toward women?

The second reason bias is difficult to establish is that the sources of bias may not be aware of it, and even if they are, it is almost certain they are not going to openly admit it. In other words, bias is rarely going to be verified at its source. These two reasons why it is difficult to identify bias (disagreement and difficulty of verification) clearly contribute to the problem we are facing here—trying to discern whether there is evidence of bias in who receives a death-penalty verdict. This has not prevented the open assertion of such, especially in the case of racial prejudice. Since suspected racial bias has a substantial emotional component in our contemporary society that may limit reasoning and consideration of alternatives, assertions of racial prejudice can last a long time without serious challenge.

If it is difficult to prove that capital punishment decisions are or are not biased, the choice may be to simply ignore the assertion. Sometimes, however, the evidence at issue makes too strong a case to ignore. That means if an alternative to bias is to be considered, it becomes necessary to do what is often so difficult. One must identify a reasonable alternative to bias as an explanation, probably from the criminal circumstances, and then look for evidence to support the alternative. That is precisely what was done in discussing whether racial bias and gender bias can play a role in determining who receives the death penalty.

Racial Bias in Awarding the Death Penalty

One of the most publicized assertions of routine racial bias in a state criminal justice system involved a study of sentencing for murder in Georgia (Baldus, Pulaski & Woodworth, 1983). The judgment of these researchers in their published paper, that the deep-south Georgia courts harbored a serious bias against blacks, met very little challenge. In fact, it was subsequently reiterated in 1987 by the Supreme Court in yet another incursion into social practices in this country that had become woven into the fabric of American law.

The Baldus group (hereafter referred to simply as "Baldus") raised the issue of whether a sentencing bias against blacks existed in Georgia prosecution of capital murder. The researchers may well have chosen Georgia to seize the opportunity to reveal racial prejudice in the courts. It did have a history of racial inequality as a deep-south state. The statistics that were disclosed by his investigation encouraged Baldus to interpret his findings as evidence of prejudice. The Baldus study sampled the records of over 2000 murder cases in the Georgia courts and found that the death penalty was handed down in 22% of the cases where blacks had killed whites, 8% where whites had killed whites, 3% where whites had killed blacks, and 1% where blacks had killed blacks. The fact that these percentages came from a state with a deep-south heritage of white superiority to black lent itself to what must have seemed like two obvious conclusions for the researchers. One was that white lives were deemed more valuable than black lives. Taking a more valuable life should result in more severe punishment. This conclusion seemed to be corroborated by these percentages in several ways. The most striking corroboration appears in the findings that 22% of the blacks who took a white life received the death penalty, but only 1% of the blacks who killed blacks received this sentence.

The second conclusion regarding racial bias that can be drawn from the Baldus percentages has to do with the race of the offender. Look at those percentages again. If a black crossed the racial divide by taking a more valued white life, the chances were about 1 in 4 that the offender would draw a death penalty. If a white took a more valued white life, the probability was only about 1 in 12 that capital punishment would result. This could suggest that when a black murders across race in victimizing a white that a greater punishment is more likely to be exacted for two reasons—the black race of the offender and the white race of the victim.

An assumption of racial bias in assigning the death penalty in the Georgia courts gained impetus nationally when it served as the basis for petition to the Supreme Court in 1986. The petition alleged that Warren McCleskey, a black man who was sentenced to be executed after being convicted of murdering a white victim, had been deprived of his Eighth and Fourteenth Amendment rights because of racial discrimination in a Georgia court. The Baldus study was cited as the centerpiece of the appeal. A Supreme Court ruling by the narrowest of margins, a 5–4 vote, went against the appeal but did not challenge the study or its interpretation of the evidence. It was rejected by the majority because they were uncertain that racial bias played a part in this particular case. However, justices offering dissenting opinions were not all that reticent about assuming racial bias in the Georgia courts based upon the Baldus study. The dissenting justices excoriated the state's capital punishment procedures. We are still exposed to the occasional media echoes of these mid-1980s assumptions made by researchers and justices alike.

Some years after the Baldus study and the Supreme Court minority affirmation were published, two students and I collaborated in an investigation that considered some alternatives to racial prejudice as explanations for the Baldus findings (Heilbrun, Foster, & Golden, 1989). Without going into agonizing detail, I shall offer the gist of our findings. We worked with information from a near-complete sample of men who were on death row following capital murder conviction in Georgia courts. Dangerousness-index scores were obtained from the prisoners. This index has received our attention before as an extensively validated risk measure of violence. Remember, having the scores gave us something other than the crimes committed as an independent measure of dangerousness. If we had depended on their crimes for gauging dangerousness, all prisoners would have looked the same, since they all committed capital murder.

Our results most relevant to the Baldus findings involved a comparison in dangerousness between blacks who killed whites (interracial murder) and subsequently received the death penalty and whites who killed whites (intraracial murder) and then received the same sentence. You probably recall the Baldus results, but I will summarize them selectively in case you do not.

You may recall that 22% of the interracial black murderers were sentenced to die and only 8% of the intraracial white murderers received that verdict. The Baldus group concluded, after examining these percentages and comparing them to those involving black victims (1–3% death-penalty sentences), that the Georgia courts considered the white lives more valuable and levied the death punishment more frequently if a white were victimized. Following the Baldus line of reasoning, the especially high percentage of blacks killing whites found on death row could be explained by two types of prejudice that cast the black murderer as an inferior and the white victim as superior. The black who chose a white victim would be the target of maximum racial prejudice. Thus the very high 1 out of 4 receiving the death penalty.

In the Heilbrun, Foster and Golden study we looked at the dangerousness of this black interracial murderer on death row and at a possible alternative explanation for the relatively high percentage of capital convictions. Blacks who murdered whites were far more dangerous than whites who murdered white victims and ended up on death row. This means that the larger representation of black interracial murderers among those on death row in Georgia need not require an exclusive assumption of bias. The black interracial murderers considered as a whole scored as dangerous enough to have gained death-row status on their own without assuming they were sent there by deep-south prejudice. Keep in mind that the dangerousness index was validated by showing, among other things, that higher scores predicted more brutal violence. Furthermore, excessive brutality of a murderer is a mainstay of the death-penalty statutes in Georgia.

Some unreported data from the 1989 Heilbrun, Foster, and Golden study were belatedly analyzed and reported the following year (Heilbrun, 1990). These results help to confirm the conclusion that greater dangerousness represents one of the reasons why the death-penalty sentence was so frequently handed down to blacks who killed whites in Georgia. The following sequence of relationships was being considered. These black murderers tested out as especially dangerous; especially dangerous men commit the most serious acts of violence; the most serious acts of violence are more likely to be sentenced to capital punishment.

The 1990 study included a sample of over 200 men who had been convicted of murder in the Georgia courts. These included the death-row murderers from the previous study and a larger sample of murderers who received a life sentence. The purpose of the study was to further analyze the tested dangerousness scores of these men, all of whom had taken a life. Neither race of the offender nor race of the victim was considered. Dangerousness index scores in this analysis were related to two circumstances of the murders they had committed. Both circumstances could contribute to the perceived ruthlessness of the act in the eyes of the jury. One was whether the victim was a woman or a man; killing a woman would be considered more ruthless. The second circumstance was the judged cruelty of the act itself taken from the description of the crime which was found in the prison file. The combination of four variables in the results makes interpretation cumbersome, so I shall offer a table presenting the findings.

I should preface any interpretation of the Table 5 results with some explanation of the numbers and what they mean along with the variables being related on the table. Two numbers appear. The number (N) in each group and the mean (average) score on the dangerousness index for each group.

Table 5
Dangerousness of Murderers Considered by
Rated Cruelty of the Crime, Sex of the Victim,
and the Sentence Received by the Criminal

Sentence	Cruel Murder of a Female Victim		Cruel Murder of a Male Victim		Murder of a Male or Female Victim without Cruelty	
	N	Mean	N	Mean	N	Mean
Death Penalty	31	2902	22	2433	22	2490
Life Sentence	17	2400	26	2229	83	2394

Note: the average dangerousness index score is set at 2500 for the entire sample of murderers

All that needs to be understood about the index score is that the average score for the entire sample of murderers is set at 2500. If a group score falls above that figure it means that subset of criminals is more dangerous than average for this sample. Keep in mind that the sample is made up of very dangerous men—murderers, many of whom have received the death penalty. Accordingly a subset average above 2500 identifies these men as extremely dangerous even when compared to a lofty standard of dangerousness.

Cruelty of the murder was rated by judges in the study after examining the criminal circumstances in the prisoner's file. As you might guess, both excessive cruelty of the crime and killing a female victim are given weight in assigning the death penalty.

The conclusion from Table 5 may now seem obvious. Men who killed a woman in a particularly brutal way were the most likely to receive the death penalty—about 65% (31 out of 48) of these men did in this sample. The same men received a singularly high average dangerousness-index score (2902). Murderers who presented any other combination of victim gender or cruelty were less likely to receive a capital punishment verdict, 46% (22 out of 48) down to 21% (22 out of 105). These remaining subsets also received comparable average dangerousness scores (2229–2490) that were on the low side for this sample of murderers.

Take notice of what these follow-up results mean with regard to the Baldus findings. Very dangerous men, black or white, are more likely to act on homicidal impulse in such a way as to invite capital punishment. Black men who killed white victims in Georgia proved very dangerous by independent test. The seemingly obvious conclusion of courtroom prejudice that was used to explain the Baldus percentages is becoming less obvious as black interracial murderers emerged as exceedingly dangerous men even by death-penalty standards.

Perhaps the evidence being presented as an alternate explanation for seeming bias in sentencing black interracial murderers to capital punishment in Georgia courts is sufficient at this point to allow me to comment on the evidence/morality issue central to this book. The Baldus percentages were automatically cast in an unfavorable light by treating them as a violation of a moral standard—unbiased litigation, fairness of trial. It did not require the collection of additional hard-to-get evidence nor did it require any further complicated reasoning. It is little wonder that even brilliant legal scholars on the Supreme Court would jump on the moral bandwagon. These justices are not tutored in scientific inference and probably not committed to considering criminal dynamics in forming their opinions. That much is evident in their earlier consideration of capital punishment.

Back to the world of evidence again regarding the issue of racial bias in assigning the death penalty. There is more to come! A second approach to considering the nature of the crime as an alternative to courtroom bias in explaining the

Baldus percentages was apparent in a study I conducted some years later (Heilbrun, 1996). The trial phase of a capital case considers the guilt or absence of guilt for the defendant and emphasizes the evidence relevant to the commission of the crime. During the second phase the issues of mitigating and aggravating circumstances have to be weighed in order to consider whether the crime merits the death penalty or some lesser punishment, probably LWP. Two such aggravating circumstances were introduced in the previous section—cruelty involved in the crime and the male offender's choice of a female victim.

Let me start to describe the 1996 study by going a bit deeper into the meaning of terms as they apply to circumstances in the penalty phase. Mitigating factors such as an argument with a friend are those that make a crime less objectionable and more readily understood. Aggravating factors are those that make a crime an even more grievous act such as victimizing a child, but degree of brutality or cruelty seems to be the most salient consideration in determining aggravation.

Credit is due J. L. Katz (1987) who, to the best of my knowledge, was the first to openly challenge the Baldus study and its interpretation of bias. He testified in federal court on the matter in the same year as the Baldus data were published. Katz examined the case records of men in Georgia convicted of murder, showing special interest in the section describing the circumstances of the crime. He found that homicide cases in which the victims were white involved more grievous behavior, whether the offenders were black or white. Cases in which whites were victimized were described by Katz as "more likely to involve other offenses, such as armed robbery, kidnapping, or rape. They were more likely to be brutal, with higher rates of mutilation, torture, and clubbing or stomping the victim to death. And they were more likely to be cold-blooded, with the assailant motivated, for example, by the pursuit of money or the necessity to silence a witness to a crime."

Katz concluded that his observations, abstracted from prison files, helped explain the higher rates of death-penalty sentences for the murder of whites reported by Baldus. Excessive brutality along with multiple felonies were sufficient aggravating factors to explain a higher rate of capital punishment for killing a white victim without involving the assumption that greater value was placed on a white life in the deep-south Georgia courts.

Yet the alternative interpretation for the Baldus percentages with regards to white victims in general is only part of the story as far as the present discussion goes. There is still the matter of the higher percentage of blacks than whites who received the death penalty after being convicted of murdering white victims. Katz in further testimony had suggested that the answer might be found in the absence of mitigation (along with the excess of aggravation) for the black perpetrator. There were fewer reasons to take a less harsh view of the crime. The lack of personal closeness between blacks and whites in and around the 1980s could help explain this. Mitigation of a crime tends to be enhanced when the criminal and victim are closer in a social sense.

Evidence was lacking in the earlier studies in which I was involved as far as establishing the social relationships between the offender and victim by racial identity. One problem in pursuing this was the virtual absence of cases in which a white offender had killed a black victim. However, our data did allow us to consider the question of social closeness and mitigation between two of the racial pairings: blacks who murdered whites and blacks who murdered blacks. You will recall that these two pairings fell at the extremes of the Baldus percentages regarding capital punishment. Some 22% of the black-on-white murderers received the death penalty, and only 1% of the black-on-black murderers were given that sentence. Considering those extremes accomplished one thing for certain. If a difference between these death-penalty percentage extremes cannot be found in what is supposed to be a mitigating factor, then the supposition that social closeness is a mitigating factor must be wrong. Blacks who killed blacks have to be more closely related socially to the victim than blacks who killed whites or no case can be made for closeness of relationship in mitigating the death penalty.

The procedure involved having research judges make ratings from the information in prisoner files on a four-point scale of social closeness: the offender and the victim were strangers, acquaintances, friends, or family. The analysis of the ratings verified the observation made by Katz. The average rating for black-on-black murder fell between "acquaintance" and "friend" on the scale. This average for black-on-white murders fell almost at the "stranger" point of the scale. Whatever mitigation of the murder is offered by some degree of close relationship to the victim was clearly lacking when a black engaged in an interracial killing of a white victim. So we have yet another factor associated with intentional killing and subsequent capital conviction that makes it less necessary to conclude that there was racial bias in the Georgia courts. In fact, this review of evidence concerning what appeared to be obvious racial bias in extending the death penalty to blacks who murdered white victims in deep-south Georgia leads me to question whether systematic bias was present at all.

Gender Bias in Awarding the Death Penalty

Useful information concerning possible bias in the capital punishment of women was reported by the Death Penalty Information Center of Southern Methodist University. They state that only around 3% of the total number of executions in preexisting settlements and subsequently in the United States between 1608 and 2002 have been women. Capital punishment had been near a male monopoly for about 400 years. This figure certainly raises the question of whether the death penalty has been subject to bias favoring women (or antagonistic to men).

If the execution count by gender is restricted exclusively to a more contemporary period, the picture does not change much. In fact, it becomes even more one-sided. The Death Penalty Information Center found that about 1 in 10 murder arrests in this country were accounted for by women in the period following restoration of the death penalty, 1977–2002. The Department of Justice crime statistics used in my deterrence study that looked at single offender/single victim homicides put this ratio at 1 in 8 murder arrests for women relative to men in this same time period. Compared to the 3% female execution figure over 400 years this 9–11% range of murder arrests sounds like an equalitarian trend.

However, as the woman proceeds through the criminal justice system after her arrest for murder, the gender ratios begin to change radically. The Information Center tells us that only 1 in 52 death sentences following capital prosecution involved a woman, about 2%. Only 1 in 74 inmates found on death row was female, reducing the presence of women to 1–2%. When it came to actual execution just 1 woman for every 88 men was put to death, about 1%. Police investigation confirmed a paucity of women thought to be involved in intentional killing. Nevertheless, the remaining steps in consummating a capital prosecution exposed a progressive winnowing down to a very few adult females that are executed.

There are two ways of attempting to explain the very lopsided ratios of women to men who are arrested for murder, undergo capital prosecution, receive the death penalty, and are actually executed. One approach directs attention to the behaviors and social roles that females tend to adopt as they are socialized into adulthood. The focal interest in this approach would be concerned with whether these markers of female personality have a bearing upon the occurrence of criminal behavior, particularly violence, and the form that violence might take. This analysis would have less to do with bias in the criminal justice system and more to do with whether female predisposition will affect participation in violent crime and the type and circumstances of any violent criminality that they will display. In short, the emphasis would be on the woman's habit structure and not so much on being perceived by others as a woman.

The second approach to explaining the disproportionate ratios would have to do with how other people are disposed to deal with women in general as contrasted with how they deal with men. This would include the attitudes and expectations held about the female gender, the behaviors and roles that are seen as appropriate for women, and, in the present context, various actions and conditions that seem inappropriate to impose upon a woman. "Chivalry" has been used to describe those specific attitudes and expectations that protect women from being held to the same standard of punishment as men in our criminal justice system. While this term conjures up images of medieval knights and helpless damsels in distress, I have no problem in believing that females are still protected to some extent in our society, feminists to the contrary.

Rather than spending time trying to prove what may seem obvious, that to some extent women behave differently and are treated differently than men, I will get right to the point, summarized in this way. Do women behave differently from men in the conduct of their crimes in such ways as to reduce the probability that they will ever be subjected to the death penalty? That will be recognized as an inquiry into how much the female/male discrepancy in capital punishment can be attributed to the differences in gender-related criminal behavior. After presenting research relevant to answering that question as best as I can, we will then consider evidence regarding whether women, once in the criminal justice system, will be treated more leniently than men. At that point we will be considering what is more readily identified as gender bias. The discussion will be preceded by two warnings. For one, it is never possible in this discussion to separate gender-related behavior and gender bias. What women do and how they are perceived sometimes defy separation.

The second warning to bear in mind is that research on the behavior of women or the treatment of women relevant to capital punishment would not be practicable without being granted some leeway in the effort. The ever-dwindling and nearly nonexistent percentages that were cited previously should make it clear that research samples would be too limited in number if proximity to execution were required for subject selection. What shall be presented are studies of women who have engaged in violent crimes other than capital murder as well as nonviolent crimes for comparison. Hopefully, generalizing from serious violence to the most serious of violent crimes will prove informative even if cautiously presented.

We will begin by considering the nature of female criminal violence relative to that of males and how this might relate to the paucity of women facing a death penalty. A study of crimes committed by women and men (Heilbrun, 1982) focused upon the degree of impulsivity or premeditation of the criminal act. You will recall that I have emphasized the *intentionality* of the killing in making use of the murder statistics reported by the Department of Justice. That is how murder (and non-negligent manslaughter) were defined—as involving intentional killing of another person. It is also true that the justice systems look upon the distinction between impulsive and premeditated as a critical feature distinguishing murder from other types of lethal violence. Vehicular homicide, for example, represents a violent crime for which the person is held responsible. Premeditation would be minimal and punishment limited. Conviction for capital murder without proving intent to kill would probably be close to impossible in our legal system.

The 1982 study had judges rate the impulsiveness or premeditation for the crimes committed by about 600 females and 600 males that had led to their imprisonment between 1955 and 1978. These ratings were made by research judges, based on the description of each prisoner's crime found in the prison files. The ratings were made on a four-point scale extending from "clearly not planned and clearly a spontaneous act" (value = 1) to "clearly planned and clearly not a spontaneous act" (value = 4). Rating averages revealed a clear distinction between women and men. Violent crimes involving physical aggression (murder, manslaughter, assault) revealed a clear tendency toward spontaneity for women with average ratings between 1.50 and 1.95. These averages for men were considerable higher, ranging between 2.32 and 2.56 toward the premeditated end of the scale.

The crime of robbery is classed as a violent crime by criminologists. This is somewhat arbitrary, however, since it does not involve physical aggression, only the threat of it. Crimes involving robbery along with other crimes defined as nonviolent (burglary/theft, forgery, drug offenses) were rated on the scale as far more premeditated and less spontaneous than violent offenses involving physical aggression. One interesting thing about this second grouping of crimes is that female crimes were all rated on average as more premeditated (3.44–3.91) than those committed by males (3.16–3.36).

Conclusions? Women are considerably more impulsive than men in violent crimes involving physical aggression toward the victim. This was most apparent in cases of murder for women (average rating = 1.50) and men (average rating = 2.51). Ratings for crimes not involving physical violence revealed the woman to be slightly more premeditated than a man. This reversal wards off the assumption that females are loath to commit crimes in general and do so only on the spur of the moment. It is physical aggression, especially murder, that is anathema to women and seemingly does not fit readily into their criminal premeditation.

These results and observations deserve our attention because capital murder represents the ultimate in lethal violence involving physical aggression toward a victim. The results of the 1982 ratings study would lead us to expect that murder, should it be perpetrated by a woman, would lack the premeditation required to be prosecuted successfully as a capital case.

Perhaps one more line of investigation may be enough to make the point that female violence, actually aggressive enough to kill, is less likely to merit capital punishment than would be true for a male. This evidence will bear upon the mitigation/aggravation factor in the penalty phase of a capital trial (Heilbrun, 2006). The Justice Department's annual report on crime in this country reveals a remarkable similarity in one aspect of murder as committed by women and men over a 26-year period (1997–2002). It is open-season on men as victims for both sexes. More than 80% of the murders committed by women during this span targeted a male, and 73% of the male murderers victimized another male. Victims ranged in age from mid-adolescence to adult in almost every case.

Comparable high percentages of male victims was about the only similarity between murders committed by the two sexes, however. Thirty-six cases were selected from our prior study on gender differences in criminal impulsivity/premeditation in which a woman murdered a man. In 20 of those cases (56%) there was a history of the woman being battered by the eventual male victim. While I lack a reliable figure of the prevalence of battering by the male in the usual adult heterosexual relationship, I would be surprised if it were nearly that high. It would be a reasonable conclusion, then, that these female murderers tended in substantial number to be responding to prior aggressive provocation and would be able to claim the man's abuse as a mitigating factor. This would further reduce the odds of receiving the death penalty even if the state chose capital prosecution. Men rarely claimed to have been abused by the victim of their homicide.

The second approach to considering bias that I want to consider by using actual evidence has to do with choices seeming to favor females once they enter the criminal justice system. Up to this point we have discussed how factors such as impulsivity (lack of intent) of the criminal and provocation by the male victim reduce the chances that a woman will have to contend with capital punishment. These factors evolve from female gender attributes such as aversion to physical aggression and vulnerability to abuse by a male. Now I would like to concentrate on crimes that fall short of capital murder in severity to see if any pattern is apparent that would suggest that bias may exist in the treatment of women after they are convicted of lesser crimes and sent to prison.

Data from the 1982 Heilbrun study not previously covered in this section gives us the amount of time women and men spend in prison for the same nominal crimes; for example, how long would each gender stay incarcerated given a manslaughter conviction? Time in prison is to be understood as determined by two things—the length of the original sentence (possible courtroom bias) and timing of release (possible parole-board bias).

It was found that men averaged more time in prison than women for the same nominal crime in six out of seven comparisons. The differences in average time for men were 32%–59% longer for manslaughter, murder, and forgery offenses and 103%–107% longer for burglary/theft, robbery, and assault. The genders were about even in time spent in prison for drug offenses. The analysis failed to consider the specific circumstances of each crime, so it is possible that male criminal behavior is routinely more deserving of longer sentences or delayed release. The best that can be said is that whatever the crime was called and whether it was violent or nonviolent, the woman was usually punished less in terms of time in prison for committing it than was the case for a man. It also seems worth noting that release from prison via the parole route, as was commonly the case, entails the question of public safety that must concern the parole board. By my experience women would more readily qualify favorably in this regard. If that is true then the question remains whether the gender difference is a matter of bias or the parole board is just doing its job of protecting the public. It seems more the latter.

Perhaps the best conclusion that can be drawn from the various sources of evidence on gender differences in crime and punishment is that there is some bias favoring women all down the criminal justice line. Having said that it must be added that some of these differences are more apparent than real. This is clearest in the case of capital murder. The very few women subjected to execution can be explained in large measure by female personality traits that limit the possibility of intentional killing, especially under egregious circumstances.

A final observation is in order. The dwindling percentages of women in transition through the justice systems of this country as suspects in a capital murder case and the almost nonexistent percentage subjected to execution find substantial if not total explanation in the way that females are acculturated into adulthood. The same thing can be said for courtroom behavior in deep-south Georgia in the 1970s and 1980s. When enough trouble was taken to examine the circumstances of capital cases in which there was a concentration of death-penalty verdicts for blacks who murdered white victims, the obligatory conclusion of racial bias began to fade. This does not mean that individual bias never occurred favoring women or disparaging blacks: only that criminal justice systems seem to be able to do their jobs without routine collective bias.

Chapter 6

Summary, Conclusions, and Post-script

The primary purpose of the study described in this book was to acquire credible evidence concerning whether capital punishment serves as a deterrent to the criminal act of intentional killing. The results of the investigation seem conclusive. Evidence bearing directly upon the issue indicates that the death penalty does deter willful killing in the United States. The direct evidence finds support in a number of ancillary analyses of the data. Research design for the investigation proved valuable for testing deterrence value of capital punishment, fully defined in terms of both inhibition and disinhibition. The design also allowed some less well understood and infrequently cited parameters of these processes to be clarified.

Primary Conclusion

The primary conclusion drawn from the evidence was that the presence of death-penalty statutes in a state is associated with the deterrence of intentional killing in that state. Deterrence was evident in the marked increase in willful killing when capital punishment was compromised by legal action and by further increase in willful killing when capital punishment was totally abolished. Deterrence also was found when capital punishment was legally reinstated. The restoration of death-penalty statutes was followed by a decrease of intentional killing, although the pace of reinstating inhibition was much slower than the rapid pace of disinhibition.

Ancillary Considerations

Definition of Terms

Deterrence

The dictionary defines deterrence as preventing from action by fear of consequences. A psychological definition goes beyond this by specifying two properties that must be shown by a deterrent. Inhibition, the most readily understood property, requires that the act in question is less likely to occur when the deterrent is present. Disinhibition, the second property, requires that the act is more likely to occur when the deterrent is absent. Evidence confirming both properties would strengthen the conclusion that capital punishment serves as a deterrent to intentional killing.

Extinction

The dictionary definition of extinction is causing to die out. In the deterrence study extinction as a psychological process is important in understanding the disinhibition results. When expectations that intentional killing can be and sometimes are followed by capital punishment are no longer confirmed or reinforced, these expectations begin to weaken. The stronger the expectations were initially, the longer it would take for them to extinguish. Failure of extinction means that the person would continue to expect the death penalty to be a possible consequence of intentional killing. The strength of this expectation would depend upon how well learned it was in the first place.

Theoretical Model

Any social scientist who seeks to answer questions concerning a psychological process as complex as deterrence of intentional killing would be well advised to base the work on some theoretical model. Otherwise, prediction and interpretation of results are likely to involve even more convenient guesswork than is commonly required in the abstruse work of social science.

The present study proceeded from a relatively stark theoretical foundation that sought to explain why the death penalty should have some value as a deterrent to willful killing. Most people refrain from lethal violence as a matter of conscience. Some, however, require an additional deterrent, especially under emotional conditions such as anger. Capital punishment provides an additional disincentive to lethal action, since the thought of possible execution promotes fear. Fear is an aversive emotion and can be eliminated by relinquishing the impulse to kill.

The strength of fear in this theoretical model varies with the person's awareness of two types of information. The person must be aware that capital punishment statutes even exist. Given this awareness the strength of fear is contingent upon the person's perception of how seriously the state is committed to satisfying its own death-penalty statutes. Threat provided by the death penalty, then, is a matter of degree. States that have capital punishment and, in addition, promote a keener awareness of their system by a commitment to implementing its statutes will promote more fear in those who experience an impulse to kill. States that fall short of achieving this outcome by rejecting capital punishment or, to a lesser extent, by failing to display a clear commitment to an existing system will generate less fear in someone with an impulse to kill. The less the fear, the weaker the deterrence. Other sources of individual difference in fear under conditions involving an impulse to kill and threat of execution certainly exist but were not considered in this basic theoretical model.

Research Design

The design of the deterrence study represented an effort to satisfy the major requirements of social science research—validity, reliability, consideration of variables related to deterrence but initially confounded with other data. In addition, more focused analyses were used to answer more specific questions related to deterrence.

Validity

Credibility of the primary conclusion drawn from this study, that the presence of death-penalty statutes in a state is associated with deterrence of intentional killing in that state, depends to an important extent upon how we understand deterrence. This goes beyond definition to the admission that my study, like any investigation that strives to measure deterrence of intentional killing, did not look at the prevention of the act of murder directly. Actual deterrence is a private experience to which an outsider rarely has access. It is not just that it happens within the private cognitive experience of another person. Who is going to admit openly to the deterrence of an impulse to kill? Scientific study precludes the use of inaccessible private mentation that could only be made accessible by an unreliable admission.

If actual deterrence is inaccessible for scientific research, how do we study it? The solution is to investigate the failure of deterrence which can be measured. Failure to deter is represented in the two counts that were used as dependent variables in the present research. Murder rate and absolute number of individual murders are based upon the number of times that acting on an impulse to kill has not been prevented. These counts were obtained from a reliable source—an annual Department of Justice publication that reported state by state.

The failure-to-deter counts were based on the number of intentional killings reported following police investigation and included murder and nonnegligent manslaughter crimes. This method of measuring deterrence is conservative as it underestimates the effect. A single individual may experience several impulses to kill toward one person or several people that are thwarted by fear of execution but is likely to kill no more than one. If deterrence could be measured directly, the count would be substantial because these impulses would be cumulative; measuring deterrence by its failure to inhibit an intentional killing as I did would add only one to the count. This reasoning suggests that if capital punishment demonstrates a deterrence effect in this study, it is despite the way it must be measured. This is only one of the *despite* factors that were revealed in the course of investigation. Finding proof of deterrence was an uphill struggle.

The second reason to claim validity for the deterrence results was the availability and use of temporal periods in which capital punishment was in varying stages of decline or ascendance as a viable legal entity. These successive stages of time identified periods in which the death penalty in decline would be expected to demonstrate a loss of effect or in ascendance would be expected to demonstrate a regained effect if it is actually a deterrent.

Four periods of time were examined for changes in intentional killing. A *baseline* period (1958–1967) included years in which the death penalty was coming under legal scrutiny but not yet appreciably curtailed in influence by the courts. The *moratorium* period (1968–1971) saw executions suspended in capital convictions because prosecutors feared reversal of death-penalty verdicts. Capital punishment was crippled as a legal entity but not yet dead. An *abolishment* period (1972–1976) followed upon a Supreme Court ruling that capital punishment was unconstitutional. The death penalty no longer existed. Finally, a *restoration period* (1977–2003) returned the death-penalty to legal constitutional status pending the approval of new statutes by the Supreme Court for states interested in having capital punishment.

Intentional killing numbers during the baseline period were compared with those found during the moratorium and, independently, the moratorium numbers were compared with those found during the abolishment period. These comparisons revealed what happened with respect to willful killing when the death penalty was legally compromised and then subsequently abolished altogether. Both comparisons provide evidence regarding disinhibition, one of the two effects that psychologically define a deterrent. Examination of intentional-killing counts over the 27 years following restoration of capital punishment allowed for a conclusion about inhibition, the second psychological effect required in defining a deterrent. The natural course of legal history between 1969 and 2003 allowed both elements required for defining deterrence to be examined.

Reliability

The stability of my research findings depend upon the substantial numbers of subjects upon which the results were based and the reasonably long period of time over which the deterrence effect of capital punishment was studied. The entire population of the United States was targeted for investigation, limited only by the extent to which the Justice Department does not receive police reports including all crimes of intentional killing and the United States census reports are not complete. All states were represented in the study (along with the District of Columbia).

The time covered by the study, 46 years, also promises stable results. Although the complete study was broken up into four periods, none was less than four years and extended to 27 years. The 10-year length of the baseline period was arbitrary, but the duration of the remaining periods was determined by actual circumstances within the history of American law along with the end of the study.

Possible Confounded Variables

Sometimes variables that seem extraneous to an investigation could prove to be important in determining the outcome of a study. If they are ignored, simply left buried in the mass of data (or outside the focus of analysis), important results would be masked or exaggerated. Two such variables were identified in the present study, and both proved valuable in understanding the deterrence of intentional killing. Introduction of these variables into the analysis added confidence to the primary conclusion of the study that capital punishment serves as a deterrent to intentional killing.

The first confounded variable involved a combination of two state population parameters. Considered together they identified states that were faced with a higher volume of lethal violence or, at the other extreme, states that suffered relatively little intentional killing. Total state population was one parameter and percentage of that total population represented by minorities was the other. Both were chosen as positive correlates of intentional killing. Preliminary empirical analysis verified these assumptions. More populated states with more substantial minority representation face a greater challenge than other states in their effort to deter intentional killing. Smaller states with a relatively low percentage of minorities experience the least challenge.

The second confounded variable was the seeming commitment of a state to its own capital punishment system given that it had chosen to adopt the death penalty after it was reinstated in 1977. The indicator of commitment was the number of executions for a death-penalty state that were consummated between 1977 and 2003 when the deterrence study ended. This number ranged from 1 to over 300 executions for the 27-year period and was cut as near as possible to the middle number. Those with 6 or less executions were defined as showing "weak" commitment; states with 8 or more were considered as having "strong" commitment.

The importance of commitment as a confounded variable in this deterrence study takes us back to the theoretical model. The greater the fear of execution, the more likely the person will be disinclined to act on the impulse to kill another person.

Two conditions of awareness are important to determining the level of fear. The individual must be aware that the state uses capital punishment. Beyond that, the person's perception of how vigorously the state pursues the fullest measure of capital punishment (execution) should further enhance fear and deterrence value. Said another way, if a person in a capital punishment state is aware of the death penalty for more heinous acts of lethal violence and further perceives the state as seriously committed to applying all of its statutes, there should be some deterrence of intentional killing. These conditions are met best by the strong death-penalty states.

Research Results

Preliminary analysis of the confounded variables was required in order to most clearly interpret the evidence bearing upon the primary conclusion of the study—that the death penalty serves as a deterrent to individual killing.

Confounded Variables Analyses

Population Variables

High values in total state population and minority percentage in that population were theoretically related to an elevated volume of intentional killing in that state. States with low population and minority percentage should present more reduced murder rates. States that lack corresponding high/low levels of these population parameters should fall between the extremes in willful killing.

Analysis confirmed these expectations. The evidence demonstrated a variation in murder rate from state to state depending upon these population characteristics. Consequently, analysis and interpretation concerning the deterrence of intentional killing should take differences in these population parameters into consideration. A murder-rate percentage reduction taken as evidence of inhibition in a turbulent state should be considered more of an accomplishment than the same percentage reduction in a state with less potential for lethal violence.

A relevant finding in the analysis of the population variables revealed that the states that chose to adopt the death penalty in 1977 and then demonstrated a serious commitment to its statutes were high population states with a substantial minority percentage. They faced a problem with lethal violence and did so by enlisting the threat of execution. In contrast, states that chose not to adopt capital punishment were low in population and minority percentage. These states had to contend with a less formidable obstacle in their effort to curb lethal violence and had less reason to adopt the death penalty. This would suggest that moral repugnance was not the only reason for failing to introduce capital punishment; perhaps it was not even the most important reason.

Commitment to Capital Punishment Statutes

States that adopted capital punishment differed widely in whether they implemented its statutes. Number of executions over the 27-year inhibition period (1977–2003) was used to divide these states as evenly as possible into 18 with strong death-penalty systems (8–313 executions) and 20 with weak systems (1–6 executions). To allow you to gauge the level of commitment in the weak systems, the average number of executions for these states was less than 1 every 13 years.

The purpose of this division was to establish whether a state's investment in its death-penalty system influenced the deterrence of individual killing. The theoretical model would predict that weakness of commitment would limit deterrence to some extent. Less fear would be aroused given the impulse to kill, since fewer people would even be aware of execution as a possibility and, if aware, there would more likely be a restrained perception of the state's commitment to the system. States with a strong system, however, would bring a more formidable deterrent to bear based upon its more readily recognized and more threatening character.

Perhaps it is clear after this review of the confounded variables that the determination of deterrence value is quite complex. There is not only the presence of capital punishment versus no death penalty to consider but the level of lethal violence in the state that must be kept in check and strength of the capital punishment system that would serve as the deterrent.

Capital Punishment and the Deterrence of Intentional Killing

The summary now brings us to the heart of the deterrence study. It was theoretically proposed that the death penalty in a state serves as a source of fear when the impulse to kill registers because of the possibility of being punished by execution. Blocking the impulse reduces fear and deters the homicidal act.

Two types of evidence were required to test the hypothesis that capital punishment deters willful killing. Put in the most basic terms it had to be shown that willful killing in a death-penalty state must increase when the capital punishment system is legally compromised and increase even more when the system is abolished. This would satisfy the disinhibition requirement of a true deterrent. The second type of evidence required is that willful killing in a death-penalty state must decrease when its capital punishment system is restored as a legal entity. This would meet the inhibition requirement of a true deterrent.

Disinhibition Results

The average murder rate for each of the three state groupings (strong/weak/no death penalty) over the 10 baseline years was compared with the average murder rates during the subsequent 4-year moratorium and 5-year abolishment periods. These averages were computed over all states in a group and all years in a period. Each of these three groups demonstrated a surge in murder rate when the moratorium years were compared with baseline (34.9%–55.8%). A further increase in intentional killing for all groups was registered when moratorium and abolishment averages were compared (19.2%–28.5%).

A complication was encountered, however, when the magnitude of murder increases were compared in the moratorium over baseline analysis. The no-death-penalty group of states demonstrated the highest increase in murder rate (55.8%), the strong death-penalty group the lowest (34.9%), and the states with weak systems were intermediate (45.4%). When absolute number of intentional killings were examined for disinhibition effect, there was no complication. The average absolute number of killings each year rose more radically when the death penalty was compromised in the states with strong systems (122), increased the least when the states had no death penalty (57), and the states with weak systems assumed their usual intermediate position in disinhibitory increase (89).

The same pattern of disinhibition results was apparent when the increases in murder rate and individual killing were examined for the abolishment over moratorium periods. The states with no death penalty showed the greatest increase in murder rate (28.5%), the strong group the least (19.2%), and the weak group fell in-between (23.7%). The individual murder count analysis came out as expected.

Explanation of why disinhibition effects for states that maintained a stronger commitment to capital punishment were the lowest during the moratorium and abolishment periods can be explained in learning terms. People residing in states with the death penalty develop expectations appropriate to this system of punishment. Many of these expectancies are governed by the state's investment in its system, with the likelihood of punishment and permanence of the system being among them. These expectations are learned and reinforced over the years. The stronger the learning, the harder it is to relinquish them if the death penalty is no longer viable. This process of "unlearning" is called extinction.

This proposed extinction effect allows us to understand the unexpected order of disinhibition effects. Slower extinction of expectancies would be found in states with strong capital punishment systems. This would mean that people in those states would continue to respond to some extent as though there was still a death penalty or, at least, that there would be again soon. People in states with weak systems would be expected to show more rapid extinction of expectations associated with the death penalty. The important point here is that slower extinction would limit disinhibition effect, since some people are still reacting as though the death penalty was still around or would soon be again. This would curtail disinhibition most for states with strong systems and less for states with weak systems. There should be no extinction effect for states with no death penalty. Extinction goes a long way toward explaining the order of disinhibition in states that did favor capital punishment, however.

Since extinction would not be expected to play an active role in limiting the disinhibition effect for the control group with no death penalty, the question remains why these states displayed a releasing effect simulating disinhibition at all. Several possibilities can be suggested. For one, whatever qualified as their most severe punishment in control states, substituting for the death penalty in cases involving the most egregious crimes, may not have been holding the line on deterrence of willful killing. Incarceration, probably a life sentence with parole, would have been the likely choice. Back in the late 1960s, however, when disinhibition was being measured for this study, it was not uncommon to find a "lifetime" sentence for murder dwindle considerably. I have seen incarceration as low as seven years with good behavior sufficient for parole to be considered on a life sentence. That does not qualify as much of a deterrent to intentional killing.

A second possibility for explaining the increased murder rate for the no-death-penalty states is a shift in moral tone associated with intentional killing in the general population. These are states that at least in part rejected capital punishment as a sentence on moral grounds. The Supreme Court's decisions that brought the moratorium on execution and their subsequent ruling that the death penalty was unconstitutional were not only statements on human rights but could be taken as a moral judgment on intentional killing. If a state cannot execute a criminal even for the most egregious murder without violating the criminal's rights, then how bad can intentional killing be? This reasoning may seem somewhat tortured but keep this in mind. Criminals, especially murderers, are not particularly bright or insightful. If an awareness dawns that the highest court in the land believes that no act of willful killing merits being put to death, the blameworthiness of the act may be diminished. It would not take much of a shift in permissiveness to promote a "disinhibitory" effect in the control states (see next paragraph).

Yet another contribution to the unexpected order in disinhibition effect among state groupings is more a matter of arithmetic than psychology. Only modest increases in absolute number of intentional killings were recorded in the control states during the 1968–1971 and 1972–1976 periods. However, this translated into a substantial increase in average murder rate used as a gauge of disinhibition. Since murder rates started relatively low before 1968, given the limited population parameters of no-death-penalty states, a substantial percentage increase was more readily realized. A few additional intentional killings will bring a low murder rate up in a control state using a percentage increase. This will not be true in a death-penalty state contending with a high murder rate.

Inhibition Results

The disinhibition results that have just been summarized introduced more than its share of complications. Fortunately, consideration of inhibition, the suppression of intentional killing through fear of execution, revealed more readily interpretable results.

The inhibition period under investigation began in 1977 when capital punishment was restored to constitutional favor for states interested in having their new statutes approved by the Supreme Court. Investigation continued until the end of 2003 when the deterrence study was terminated. It focused upon the same two counts of intentional killing as before—murder rate and absolute number of individual killings.

The 38 states that adopted capital punishment were separated as before into those that made a strong commitment to their systems and those that made a weak commitment. This was gauged by the number of executions that were completed between 1977 and 2003. The span of 27 years was split into three 9-year periods in order to reveal trends over time. Reestablishment of lost inhibition proved to be a very slow process after being devastated by Supreme Court decisions. Accordingly, only changes from the first third of the inhibition period (1977–1985) to the final third (1995–2003) were compared for interpretation.

It is important that we recall one of the confounded variables at this point, since it proved especially important to understanding the inhibition effect of capital punishment. This confounded variable included a pair of population parameters used in combination, total state population and percentage of that total comprised of minorities. Elevated values of both, considered in combination, were related to a high volume of lethal violence in the state. Low population parameter values in combination were related to the opposite—only a limited volume of lethal violence in the state. Both linkages were confirmed by both theory and actual measurement of intentional killing. The value of having a gauge of potential lethal violence in a state resides in establishing how formidable the task of inhibition will be for a deterrent without using the actual murder counts and engaging in circular reasoning.

Inspection of the three state groups revealed that the large population/high minority percentage states of the strong death-penalty group had the most formidable task of deterrence by inhibition, the states with no death penalty had the least formidable, and the states with weak systems of capital punishment were intermediate. The more formidable the challenge presented by a state's level of violence, the more impressive a given amount of deterrence would be.

When inhibition effect was measured by means of average murder-rate change from the first to the third 9-year period, all of the state groupings presented a decline in rate. This time, however, the average decreases in murder rate fell in the predicted order consistent with the theoretical model of deterrence. Strong death-penalty states registered a decline of 29% in murder rate when the average for the 18 states over the 1977–1985 period was compared to their average between 1995–2003. When you consider that this group of states achieved the greatest inhibition of intentional killing among all states in the country despite having to do so against the most formidable level of lethal violence in the country, it represents a significant accomplishment. This was another one of those "despite" findings.

The weak death-penalty group of states brought their average murder rate down 24% between the first and third periods. This inhibition effect was accomplished when facing a less difficult obstacle than was encountered by the strong-system states, but it still appears to be a substantial drop, especially when compared with the control grouping of states. This suggests that the separation by number of executions, the second confounded variable, did allow us to identify levels of deterrence effectiveness, a welcome addition to the theoretical model. It would appear that having capital punishment

statutes has a general inhibiting effect upon intentional killing, but states can enhance inhibition by a more dedicated
effort to satisfy its statutes. Looking ahead to the post-script at
the end of this chapter, the reader will find this observation to
be amply documented by a recent release of information.

States that did not adopt capital punishment realized a 21%
drop in murder rate from the beginning to the end of the inhibition period. The population parameters of these states showed
them to be the least dangerous in terms of intentional killing,
yet the inhibition figure was well below those accomplished
by the death-penalty states. This does demonstrate one obvious fact. There are other sources of inhibition besides the death
penalty albeit less effective.

Two other findings related to inhibition should be noted.
One involved a comparison between the murder rates during
the baseline period (1958–1967) and during the final 9-year
period in the study (1995–2003). This answered the question
of how well states with and without capital punishment had
been able to return their murder rates back down to those
existing during the halcyon years before capital punishment
was legally devastated by Supreme Court intervention. After
three to four decades of avoiding the death penalty, control
states brought their average murder rate down, but it was still
34% above their baseline average. States with a weak commitment to their capital punishment systems managed to get
their average murder rate down even more, but it remained
26% above baseline. Given a strong commitment to their systems, however, states with the death penalty returned their
average murder rate down to within 1% of this earlier level.
And remember, the 1% figure was achieved against the highest turbulence of lethal violence, the 26% figure against intermediate levels of violence and 34% in the states with the least
potential for intentional killing.

The second thing to note about inhibition of willful killing
was that it reached its zenith in this study at a time when the
incidence of nonlethal violence nationwide was increasing.

This means that at about the same time that intentional killing was being suppressed, especially in states with capital punishment, the most serious types of nonlethal violence (rape, robbery, and aggravated assault) were reported to have increased radically. This departure in trend lines suggests that capital punishment has a targeted effect upon intentional killing, as should be the case. The fear of execution is meant to home in on murder, not other forms of physical abuse. The departing trend lines for lethal and nonlethal violence in this country represents yet another example of a "despite" finding—a deterrence effect that was disclosed for capital punishment against the rising tide of serious but nonlethal violence.

Various Issues Relating to the Death Penalty

Several issues concerning the death penalty have been raised by oppositionists and discussed in this book besides the moral issue of putting people to death as a punishment for egregious criminal behavior. When these reservations are examined as criticisms of capital punishment, they often appear to be specious or contradictory. Even justified concerns appear to be resolvable.

If Capital Punishment is Abolished, What Will Replace It?

Should opposition to capital punishment result in abolishment (again!), is there a criminal penalty that could replace it? This question is rhetorical, of course, since the replacement is currently awaiting us in the wings. Life without parole is already at the disposal of juries in capital trials should a death penalty not prove to be a satisfactory verdict to the jury in the penalty phase or if a death penalty, once awarded, is subsequently adjudicated as too severe.

The lingering question, as far as I know, is whether the threat of life without parole has a deterrent effect comparable to capital punishment? What evidence was available within the present investigation casts serious doubt upon whether it does. In any case, proponents of life without parole as a replacement for the death penalty as punishment for the worst of crimes should be responsible for demonstrating comparable deterrence. The need to do so should not be dismissed by using dubious research evidence to claim that capital punishment does not deter intentional killing, thereby making comparison unnecessary.

Capital Punishment and the Problem of Irreversible Error

It has been pointed out, rightfully so, that when a prisoner is executed and subsequently evidence of innocence (or a lesser crime) is found, this erroneous death-penalty sentence cannot be corrected in a way that directly benefits the prisoner. It is not that capital cases are the only ones that risk sentencing error; this problem exists for all levels of criminal adjudication. It is just that the prisoner is no longer available for a modified sentence.

There are a couple of considerations, however, that make the problem of irreversible error, though tragic in the individual case, not a critical problem in the long run for capital punishment systems. One is that the delay in most executions following sentencing is usually very long, often 20–30 years. There has been ample opportunity for appeals based upon revision of the original evidence, new evidence, or upon erroneous trial procedure. That does not mean that unfortunate mistakes are necessarily going to be corrected by appeal, but one does wonder what the base rate of erroneous executions actually is considering the total number of capital convictions?

The second consideration is whether mistakes made in either phase of a capital trial, either in determining guilt or deciding upon the penalty, could be limited to some extent by a modification of the verdict procedure. If mistakes are being made in the trial phase of a capital case, establish a more stringent standard of guilt (with proper instructions to the jury). If you are not satisfied with the way that mitigating and aggravating factors are considered in the penalty phase, revise the weighting. Either revision, if successful, could reduce the chances of erroneous execution. A caution, however: Unduly limit the capital punishment systems through revision, and you risk the replication of the disinhibition years. An attorney-general still would dislike having a successfully prosecuted capital case reversed on appeal.

Excessive Cost of Capital Punishment

This issue is a rather puzzling one. Not so much that it registers complaint about the expense of maintaining a capital punishment system in a state but that it ignores common sense in the two types of complaint that I have seen emphasized.

It has been observed that capital trials are more expensive, sometimes far more expensive, than other types of criminal trials. Funds for indigent defendants available to the state can be devoured as defendants in capital trials are given access to expert witnesses, investigators, or defense teams comparable to the prosecution. At the same time you hear expressions of concern about irreversible errors in a capital trial. What this amounts to are two complaints about capital punishment that contradict each other. One says that trials are too expensive, and the other says that trials should be more thorough so that mistakes will be minimized. Let me see now. More thorough trials for less money? That sounds like a political statement.

The second concern that I have come across regarding the expense of capital punishment is the cost of maintaining convicted criminals under close security on death row for an extended period of time while their rights of appeal are satisfied and procrastination finally ends. If I am correct that life without parole is the heir-apparent sentence that would replace capital punishment, then the comparison in expense for verdicts reserved for the worst crimes of violence should be between these two. Life without parole as the verdict of choice would mean that the same heightened security would be required to incarcerate these most serious violent offenders, but time of incarceration would be even longer—for a lifetime. And the cost of storing prisoners in prison into their declining and terminal years is going to become increasingly expensive as aging increases psychological helplessness and physical disability. Who is going to care for these helpless and unmotivated prisoners—the security officers? Or, more likely, will additional aides be required on the geriatric prison wards at added expense?

Biased Sentencing

With something as serious as the death penalty at stake, there is good reason to be concerned about bias entering the criminal justice process at some stage—police investigation, courtroom procedure, jury verdict, appeal of the verdict. Two possible sources of bias, among many, were considered as possible problems in determining who would be exposed to the death penalty. One was race of the suspected or convicted perpetrator (black versus white), and the other was gender (female versus male).

The issue of racial prejudice in assigning the death penalty emerged in a prominent way following a study of murderers in a deep-south state (Georgia) during the 1980s. Investigators in a research study found that blacks who had been tried for killing whites were more likely to receive a capital punishment verdict than any other racial combination of murderer and victim. Bias against blacks in the deep-south seemed an obvious explanation to the researchers. The death penalty would be more likely if greater value were placed upon a white victim's life and lesser value assigned to the life of the black perpetrator. These conclusions of racial bias in the Georgia courts gained momentum when they were affirmed in the minority report of a Supreme Court case hearing an appeal from a death-row prisoner.

Considerable evidence from Georgia prison case files was collected shortly after the study of bias was analyzed. It was concluded from this evidence and other related research that the disproportionate death-penalty verdicts by race were less a matter of prejudice against blacks and more a matter of the actual nature of black-on-white lethal violence.

A second possible source of bias is suggested by the infrequency in which a woman is arrested for murder in this country(1 case out of 10) and the even more rare case of a woman who is executed for capital murder (1 case out of 88). These statistics make it seem almost certain that there is bias in the criminal justice system that serves to protect women and discriminate against men when it comes to the death penalty. Examination of the evidence collected to consider this question, however, suggested that bias did not tell the whole story. A good share of the difference between men and women in committing lethal violence and in facing capital conviction can be explained by female characteristics and how women are socialized away from violence.

These two analyses of bias suggest the importance of considering the character of behavior called for by intentional killing before concluding that prejudice has played an important role in assigning the death penalty.

Post-script

We have reached the end of the book. Looking back I hope you will agree that although the topic was a somber one, it does hold some importance for everyone. The lingering question is this. How do you get people to stop killing each other in what is supposed to be a civilized country? Perhaps the conclusion drawn from the evidence of deterrence effect for capital punishment and my own perspective on pragmatism in criminal justice has given you pause for reflection. Remember, the life you save may be your own!

Of course, the chances may seem remote that a particular individual will become one of the projected victims of intentional killing should a deterrent be lost or ineffectively implemented. Even a high murder rate such as 10 in 100,000 may not seem like much of a threat when you consider the individual case. It is only when the number of victims accumulate across a state or a nation that you might feel cause for concern over your safety. Some may be reassured by the fact that the murder rate was coming down as my study ended, especially among the states that invoked the death penalty. But as this book comes to a close, a cautionary note has been sounded with respect to capital punishment, at least for me.

Moral opposition and political skittishness are not new in the continuing effort to limit the role of the death penalty as a deterrent. This includes denial of deterrence effectiveness without considering definitive empirical evidence, I have not been reluctant to point this out in the present book. Accordingly there is no need to belabor the point here except to say that when evidence was gathered in a study having a complicated but satisfactory research design, deterrence of intentional killing was found. This was most apparent in states in which a strong death-penalty system was brought to bear upon the worst problems of lethal violence in the country. Yet in spite of having this empirical demonstration in hand, I had the occasion to come across an article posted by Wikipedia on the internet (*Capital Punishment in the United States*: 7. "Current Moratoria and de facto moratoria" updated through June 12, 2012). This survey outlined the actions of 16 death-penalty states between the reinstatement of capital punishment in 1977 and now. These may have been well-intended, but they look very much like efforts to make the death sentence fail as a deterrent.

It may not surprise you that 13 out of the 16 states that were identified as responsible for halting executions for variable periods of time were included in the weak death-penalty group of states in my investigation. Paucity of executions was the defining attribute for this grouping. Yet there were a number of possible strategies that were identified to compromise state death-penalty statutes and halt executions. Oppositionists in these 13 states must have formed a line. I will run down the list provided in the survey.

One way to halt executions is simply to ignore the fact that you have a death-penalty system. According to Wikipedia, the laws were on the books yet two states have gone through the entire period since restoration (1977–2012) without ever executing a prisoner. This says that if you do not like one of your laws, simply pay no attention to it. Two other states have held the line at one execution.

Another approach to a de facto moratorium was evident in eight other states. While all but one of these states kept their total count of executions to a minimum (1–3), they all included at least one execution on a "volunteer" basis. Seemingly this means the prisoner was given a choice and chose to die. The eighth state executed twelve prisoners and eleven of them were "volunteers." The article did not report how many prisoners refused the state's offer to put them to death as a "volunteer" as they chose to commute their own sentences. Whatever the number, common sense dictates that it involved continued incarceration despite being sentenced to die for these reluctant prisoners. What also seems clear is that the deterrence value of capital punishment has to suffer to the extent that people know that they will have a choice of getting around the verdict should they be convicted of a capital crime and await execution.

The remaining four states saw their executions held up for variable periods of time by the actions of their governor, court officials, or even their medical board. Issues relating to the method of execution (such as electrocution versus lethal injection) were commonly cited in the never-ending search for a humane way to take a life.

What is the point of dwelling on these displays of unwillingness to enforce state statutes in such a way as to counteract effective deterrence of willful killing? It is to alert the reader to the fact that all is not well in our progress toward curbing lethal violence. It is one thing to legally terminate capital punishment in a state by openly changing its laws. That requires actions that must be defended judicially or politically. It is another to maintain the system but keep throwing a monkeywrench into how it should work. In short, complaisance regarding how well we are keeping intentional killing under control is not warranted.

References

Baldus, D.C., Pulaski, C., & Woodworth, G. (1983). "Comparative Review of Death Sentences: An Empirical Study of the Georgia Experience." *Journal of Criminal Law and Criminology*, 74, 661–753.

Heilbrun, A. B. (1982). "Female Criminals: Behavior and Treatment within the Criminal Justice System." *Criminal Justice and Behavior*, 9, 341–351.

Heilbrun, A. B. (1990). Differentiation of Death-Row Murderers and Life-Sentence Murderers by Antisociality and Intelligence Measures. *Journal of Personality Assessment*, 54, 617–627.

Heilbrun, A. B. (1996). *Criminal Dangerousness and the Risk of Violence*. Lanham, MD: University Press of America.

Heilbrun, A. B. (2006). *The Death Penalty: Beyond the Smoke and Mirrors*. Lanham, MD: University Press of America.

Heilbrun, A. B., Foster, A., & Golden J. (1990). "The Death Penalty in Georgia, 1974–1987." *Criminal Justice and Behavior*, 16, 139–154.

Heilbrun, A. B., & Heilbrun, M.R. (1989). "Dangerousness and Legal Insanity." *The Journal of Psychiatry and Law*, Special reprint (Spring).

Katz, J. L. (1987, July 5). "Death Penalty Data Dispute Racial Bias Claims." *The Atlanta Journal and Constitution*.

Sellin, T. (1959). *The Death Penalty*. Philadelphia: American Law Institute.

Vila, B., & Morris, C. (1997). *Capital Punishment in the United States: A Documentary History*. Westport, CT: Greenwood Press.

About the Author

Alfred B. Heilbrun Jr. received the Ph.D. degree from the University of Iowa in 1954 and served on that university's psychology faculty from 1956 to 1965. He was awarded diplomate status in 1960 by the American Board of Professional Psychology with a specialty in clinical psychology. Dr. Heilbrun joined the faculty of Emory University in 1965 where he directed the clinical psychology training program, the university counseling service, and the community-oriented Psychological Center. Dr. Heilbrun was awarded the Walter Klopfer award from the Society for Personality Assessment in 1991 for distinguished contribution to the literature of personality assessment, and that year retired from Emory University as Distinguished Research Professor of Psychology.

Since retirement Dr. Heilbrun has been honored with the Arts and Sciences Award of Distinction by Emory College and the Graduate School of Arts and Sciences, and as a Distinguished Senior Contributor by the Division of Counseling Psychology, American Psychological Association.

He has been active as a researcher and scholar since 1956 and has included forensic psychology issues among his interests since the 1970s. Over this active period Dr. Heilbrun has been sole or primary author of over 220 scientific or scholarly publications including seven books describing his research.

www.ingramcontent.com/pod-product-compliance
Lightning Source LLC
Chambersburg PA
CBHW050524280326
41932CB00014B/2450